RENDING THE VEIL

BEGINNING THE JOURNEY OF INTIMACY WITH YOUR CREATOR

KEN ARRINGTON

To my Dad,

A beautiful testament to the essence of the Father's Heart, for which I am forever grateful

I love you

CONTENTS

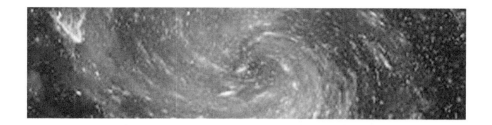

INTRODUCTION

Y ou are beginning a journey unlike any you have ever known. And all roads have brought you here. This moment. Right now.

In your hands is a simple guide designed to reveal simple concepts. And this book has one singular purpose – to draw you closer to your Creator.

To feel His heartbeat.

To know His ways.

And to reveal the truth - there is nothing between you and God. There is no veil of separation. There are no walls of your own making. There are no boundaries placed on you by institutions. And there are no borders because of man-made constructs, conditions, and regulations.

You are about to embark on an eternal journey where you will embrace *His* truth - that you were designed to walk with God. And talk with God. And see His reality in every moment of your every day. And through this intimate relationship, where prayer and union with God are as natural and as easy as breathing, you will become aware of the Glory of the Lord that covers the Earth, as the waters cover the seas.

And armed with this deep intimacy, with this love of God, you will step into your destiny, and you will change the world.

Yes. You read that right. Because of the intimate relationship you are even now developing with Christ, you will change the world.

Now don't smirk. And don't laugh. And don't doubt. The Bible says this is what you are designed for. To be not just known by Jesus, but to operate in, and TO BE IN, union with Him.

But do you notice how even reading of, and even thinking of, that kind of reality, disturbs you on some level? Sure, many of us nod and give lip service to this idea. But deep down, in your heart of hearts, do you feel like you are living that out, this reality that there is no separation between you and God? Are you seeing the manifest reality of Christ's love in your life? Is His heart for the world flowing out of you like Living Water? Is every single realm of your life manifesting the delicious fruit of the Spirit – love, joy, peace, patience, kindness, goodness, faithfulness, gentleness, and self-control?

How about from our churches? Are we Christians known for our Christ-like love and acceptance? Are we known for our compassion for others? Our servant-hearts? Our unconditional sacrifices?

Can you imagine walking into some of our houses of worship and saying *We are designed to walk and talk with God and release His love to all we encounter because we are in union with Him through Christ Jesus*?

To be sure you may hear some mumbled *Amens*, but *are we living that out?* Do our churches reflect, do we reflect ... do *YOU* reflect the sacrificial, glorious, awe-inspiring, death-defying love of Jesus?

And maybe more importantly, do you even know how to experience that love for yourself?

This book dares to believe this is possible.

Because I have seen it happen.

I have seen it happen in my life and the lives of others. I have seen this happen in the lives of people who have dared to believe that God actually did what He said He would do when He tore the veil of separation from top to bottom, physically rending the veil that symbolized the separation between God and man violently in two.

But don't let this simple book fool you.

Even though this is but a simple guide with simple concepts, I can promise you that if you contemplate what is offered here, and more importantly, put the revelations presented in this guide into practice, then you will be challenged on every level – physically, mentally, and spiritually. And if you come along with an open heart and an open mind, you will be met with revelations that will shake you to the core and transform you.

Because this book is about allowing a relationship with God to absolutely, unequivocally, radically, and literally turn your reality inside out. But in the process, you will come to see and embrace wonder unlike anything you have known in this life.

And there is no going back.

The Revelations in this guide are not designed to be simply read. They are designed to be contemplated, gnawed on, and devoured slowly. The worst thing you could do is speed-read each section and blow past it to complete the book. This is not a Bible-In-A-Year plan where you get bonus points for completing something by a certain date. Take your time. These are foundational lessons in developing radical intimacy with the Lord. Please prayerfully consider each revelation and let them soak you in His love. Each Revelation is a step on your journey, a space for introspection and transformation, to be savored over the course of a week.

At the end of each Revelation, Scriptures used or alluded to in the text will be listed. I encourage you to read through the text, to search out and examine and meditate on the Scriptures listed, and re-examine the Revelation afterward. This will help deepen your understanding and assist you in your journey of intimacy. And please, do read the Scriptures listed, as this guide will offer simple milk to get you started. But by the end, if you have put these seven Revelations into practice, you will be tasting, and daresay, even feasting upon the endless full portion of delights that God makes available to His children.

And after each Revelation, there is a section to write your thoughts down. Please do so. I cannot encourage this enough. Write down everything that comes to mind - what you are feeling, what you feel about what the Lord is saying, and what is challenging you. And make sure you save space, for this guide is designed for you to return to it after a year or so and be re-read and for you to record new responses. In doing so, you will find new kernels of truth, and you will also be able to see how much your own thought and belief practices have evolved and just how much your intimacy with the King of the Universe has deepened.

Finally, at the end of each Revelation, you will be reminded to visit the companion website, filled with immersive 3–5-minute video journeys to augment your experience, deepening your exploration of what you are learning and experiencing. This symbiosis of text and interactive digital content allows a holistic approach to spiritual growth, making these truths more than just intellectual concepts so they become lived experiences. And while it's not a requirement to complete these short journeys, they are there to encourage you, and they are designed to help you recognize and step into the realms of His love that are available to you. They may be the last bit of breakthrough that you need!

Are you ready? Do you feel the pull, the irresistible yearning for some-thing more profound, more resonant than what you've known so far in this life? If so, then realize you are now standing on the precipice, gazing into the nebulous and unknown expanse of your true reality.

These revelations will lead you on an adventure that begins with the shedding of false realities and embracing of new beginnings – a rebirth, if you will. You will come to see God not as a distant, lofty figure but as an adoring Father, ever radiant with love. And Jesus – not just as your Savior, but as your intimate Bridegroom.

You will find what it means to be a conduit between the physical and spiritual realms, to access the secret bridal chamber of the heart, to recognize the divine imprint – the gold – in every human being, and how to revolutionize your life with this newfound understanding.

But make no mistake; this is not a journey for the faint of heart. You are here because you are longing for more than what surface-level faith offers. You will be challenged. You might even be offended in some places. And you are powerful to disagree with many things that I may say. But if you're yearning to tap into the profound depths of intimacy with the King, this book can assist you. And remember, growth comes through stretching and breaking past boundaries. When pursuing intimacy with the King of the Universe, we are supposed to be uncomfortable. This is why we need the Holy Spirit, and why Jesus refers to the Holy Spirit as *The Comforter*.

So, if you're ready to pierce the surface and delve into the deep, if you're ready to disrupt, to transform, and to uncover layers of divine truth you never knew existed, then come. This is your moment. It's time to step through the torn veil.

It's time to start your journey toward an intimacy with God that transcends all understanding.

Welcome to the adventure.

REVELATION ONE

THE CURIOUS CASE OF MISTAKEN IDENTITY

L et us start with a simple question. And when you have the answer to the question, I want you to grab a pen or pencil, and write your answer down.

Got your thinking cap on?

Okay. Here we go.

Who are you?

Now, in seven words or less, use this space to write your answer down. Seven words or less to tell me who you are. That's all. And to get you started, I am going to go ahead and fill in two of the blanks for you to make it easy.

___I___ ___AM___ _____ _____ _____ _____.

Okay. Now look at your answer and make a mental note of it. Because we are going to come back to it. But first, let's talk about the question a little bit.

On the surface it *seems* like such a simple question, doesn't it?

Who are you?

Personally, I can think of a million ways to answer this question about myself. Husband, father, Jesus lover, missionary, writer, content creator, adventurer, charity director ...

But that's just scratching the surface. I can go deeper.

Am I my memories? Am I the summation of the events that have occurred in my life?

Am I my consciousness? If I was not conscious of myself as a human, would I still be a human? Would I still be me?

Is who I am defined by my ability to think, so therefore I am?

Am I a random circumstance created by arranging atoms into molecules increasing into complex organic structures?

Deep questions for sure, and we could go further. But do these answers actually answer the original question?

Who am I really?

And who are you?

While you ponder the question, I want to tell you a little more about myself. And while we're at it, we're going to take a strange detour into a discussion about a place wrapped in mystery and revelation to reveal some secrets ... about *you*.

Misapplied History

I am an avid reader and lover of history. I always have been. And my earliest memories are of cuddling up with books to shelter me from childhood traumas and fears. My childhood wasn't the happiest, but in books and stories and tales of faraway lands, I found safety. When the world and my circumstances spiraled out of my control, I could always turn to books to find escape and freedom. I was a preteen with a library card during an age when kids could be left alone in the library for hours at a time.

And there were few things I adored more.

In high school, like many other kids, I got into my first taste of trouble and ended up skipping 48 days of school during my sophomore year. But I wasn't hanging out with the cool kids smoking in bathrooms or breaking into houses. When I skipped school I spent the entire time in the library, learning about things that I actually cared about, instead of what I thought I was wasting my time with in school.

Strange, I know. But hey. I gotta be me.

And I spent most of those long library days reading tales of King Arthur and his famous Knights of the Round Table. The stories of brave knights, adventures, magic, and fantastic places lit my young mind on fire. And as I grew into my university years in pursuit of a degree in English Lit, I came to regard Sir Thomas Malory and Alfred, Lord Tennyson, the sources of many Arthurian tales, as primary inspirations for my burgeoning writing career.

So, you can imagine my glee twenty years later when I had the chance to explore Caerleon, Wales, a place that for almost 1,500 years was physically linked to King Arthur and his Round Table.

Caerleon is located in South Wales, just a stone's throw from the border of England, and sits right outside Newport, the 3rd largest city in Wales.

But far removed from the sounds of city life, stepping onto the soft windswept hills of Caerleon is like walking into a hazy dream. There is a sense of walking through history in this place, as if just a few feet underground thousand-year-old stories are waiting to be unearthed and told. Because underneath the quaint and quiet green rolling landscape of Caerleon lay the archaeological ruins of a legendary fortress that 2,000 years ago housed over *thirty-thousand* soldiers, and was the launching point for a 400-yearlong invasion of Britannia.

The hollow mound at Caerleon, as it exists today

Once leaving Caerleon's sleepy town center and following the walking trails southwest, you'll quickly come across a curious site that has mystified people for over 1500 years. A massive hollow oval mound, longer than a football field and dug deep into the ground, greets the curious, with strange stone outcroppings and what appears to be the foundation stones of ancient seating ringing the perimeter. Lush green grass fed by constant Welsh rains covers the ground and the hills, and the cool morning mist floats above the strange structure beckoning of its secrets to the casual passers-by.

For centuries, this massive oval mound cut into the earth has been a source of wonder and mystery. And like many strange and mysterious sites in South Wales, this curious location has been linked to the most well-known king of Britain – King Arthur.

For hundreds of years, long-held legends and rumors of this site being the home of King Arthur and his Round Table were widespread and passed down orally, and in the 12th century, Geoffrey Monmouth in his History of the Kings of Britain wrote that indeed, Caerleon was the site where Arthur was named King of Britain, and it was here that the Round Table of Camelot made its home. And in 1191 AD, Gerald of Wales in his Itinerarium Cambriae, wrote of Caerleon, "the Roman ambassadors here received their audience at the court of the great king Arthur."

The idea that Caerleon was the ancient site of King Arthur's Camelot was so common, that 300 years later an invading French army diverted from their path of conquest to visit the large oval mound so they could pay homage to the legendary king. And for 800 years the Arthurian story of this locale was believed to be an established fact, and there were few doubts about its authenticity. Later Arthurian writer Thomas Malory claimed Arthur's capital wasn't at Caerleon but it was where he was re-crowned as High King of Britain. Alfred Tennyson, author of the classic Arthurian tale, *Morte d'Arthur,* wrote his work while residing in Caerleon at The Hanbury Arms in the mid-19th century.

For almost 1500 years it was widely accepted as a factual truth that Caerleon was intimately connected to King Arthur. But the truth had very little to do with the fabled king and his court.

Excavations in 1909 revealed Caerleon was once the site of the Roman military city of *Isca Augusta*, the legendary legionary fortress that dominated South Wales between 74 and 410 AD. And the mysterious oval mound? It wasn't home to King Arthur's Court. It was the foundation of a massive Roman amphitheater that for over 300 years hosted animal hunts, gladiator battles, and military parades for the invading Romans.

At Caerleon's height of power, the walls of the amphitheater were over 30 feet high and provided seating for up to 6,000 spectators. And over 30,000 Roman soldiers lived, breathed, ate, and trained at Isca Augusta at a time, using the fortress as a launching point for Roman invasions throughout South Wales over 2000 years ago.

The ampitheater of Isca Augusta (now Caerleon) circa 200 AD

But after the Romans departed Caerleon in 410 AD, without the might of Rome able to continue upkeep on the fortress, it fell into disuse. And over the centuries, nature reclaimed the once mighty administrative buildings, barracks, baths, and amphitheater, hiding the city and its paved streets beneath layers of soil and lush green grass.

For almost *1500 years*, the full truth of Caeleon's history was hidden, with false histories and labels attached to it, until that false history became Caerleon's reality.

Until 100 years ago, when those who wanted to explore Caerleon's mysteries deeper than surface level, and who had the skills to do so, began to explore what was underneath ... and worked to bring its truth to the surface, revealing Caerleon's true identity to the world as a Roman fortress and amphitheater, and not the location of a mythical king of Britain.

The Truth About Your Identity

Now you might not be that big into history. And that's okay. But, in understanding the false *and* the true history of Caerleon, there is a foundational lesson for you in developing your understanding and intimacy with God.

There is a YOU that you *think* you know.

But the truth is, there is a YOU that was created before time began - the YOU that you truly are.

And since you have been born, the world has sought to qualify you, quantify you, categorize you, and define you. You have been given labels, types, and names. Other people, not knowing the real YOU, have come along and placed their version of you upon you. You have even adopted many of these worldly ideas as YOUR identity, and you've come to accept those identities as who YOU are. You have created molds and masks around these ideas, and adapted yourself to them, taking on the appearance of these identities and accepting them as your own.

But the real you ... YOU are so much more. YOU are more than a label, your job, or your position. You are more than a partner. You are more than a parent or child. You are more than your greatest success. And more than your greatest failure.

When you allow the world to define you, when you accept its identities and labels and classifications as your own and define yourself by them, then you are subject to the whims of the world.

You are susceptible to the weight of your false identity.

Just like Caerleon, you are misidentified. And your history? Well ... it's wrong. And sure, that false history may seem great, and may even lean into who you are a little bit, but at its heart, it's a lie keeping you away from the full truth of who you are.

And when you are defined by the world, the world WILL overwhelm you, overweigh you, and when you don't suit its purposes, will crush you. And when the world is done with you, it will bury you six feet deep. And then overgrow you.

Just like what happened at Caerleon.

But what if?

What if the world didn't define you? What if you were actually defined by a Higher Power?

What if there was a Father who called you to be more, who called you to live your truest identity in whom He created you to be? Who created you to be loved by him, and to walk with him, and talk with him, and who has called you to creatively and positively transform this world by demonstrating him – to define the world with *his* glory, instead of the other way around? *To be fruitful and multiply and fill the earth and subdue it, and have dominion over the fish of the sea and over the birds of the heavens and over every living thing that moves on the earth – Gen1:28*

And what if there is a Son, whose sole purpose when He walked upon this Earth was to reveal the love of that Father to children who had lost their way, children who had let the crushing weight of the world define them and their view of the Father?

What if there is a Son who revealed a way back to the heart of that loving Father, opening the Heavens and rending the veil, revealing to a broken world the truth about the Father's love and devotion?

What if the Son revealed to the Father's children their true worth and power, giving the world, who had defined God as angry and absent for so long, the real and true picture of God? *For if you have seen the Son, then you have seen the Father -John 14:9*

And what if you dared to believe that everything you just read is absolutely true?

You see, who you think is YOU, is not.

The true YOU can only be defined by the one who created YOU – your Creator.

The true you is loved and cherished, no matter what you think you have done or how low you think you have gone. To a loving father, the son or a daughter is *always* a son or a daughter, no matter what the son or daughter has done.

The true YOU is not, could not, be a lowly worm, an unworthy wretch, or any of that other misidentified garbage. Because if the worth of something is established by the price paid for it, Heaven paid the ultimate price to restore your true identity to you.

You were created with purpose, with passion, and with love. And while the pain of this world has done all it can to take those things away, the Father offers you another way back - the way of peace, the way of shalom, the way of acceptance and nurturing and love.

But how do you step into that realization? How do you leave behind what the world says is YOU? How do you dig back through the overgrowth, the false belief, and the implied identities that the world has shouldered upon you?

To find out who you truly are and enter the kingdom that is yours *by right*, in the words of a Being infinitely wiser than I, you must be *born again*.

Embracing The Mystery of Being Born Again

The phrase *being born again* has become quite popular, hasn't it?

You see it plastered on billboards, social media posts, and church banners – *Come and get born again and wash your sins away!*

However, I can't help but believe that billboards and Sunday gatherings weren't necessarily what Jesus had in mind.

Somewhere along the way, we have lost something in our understanding of being born again. By turning it into a catchphrase, we have overlooked the deeper meaning that Jesus intended when He used these words in a conversation with one of the most knowledgeable men of His time. The concept of being born again is a mystery that baffled the wise and even those well-versed in the Scriptures:

> *"Most assuredly, I say to you, unless one is born again, he cannot see the kingdom of God." Nicodemus said to Him, "How can a man be born when he is old? Can he enter a second time into his mother's womb and be born?" Jesus answered, "Most assuredly, I say to you, unless one is born of water and the Spirit, he cannot enter the kingdom of God. That which is born of the flesh is flesh, and that which is born of the Spirit is spirit. Do not marvel that I said to you, 'You must be born*

again.' The wind blows where it wishes, and you hear the sound
of it, but cannot tell where it comes from and where it goes. So
is everyone who is born of the Spirit" – John 3:3-8

Now, let's unpack this.

Imagine the scene. Jesus is speaking to Nicodemus, not just any Pharisee, but a member of the Sanhedrin, the influential ruling council of the Jewish faith. Nicodemus held a prestigious position and was considered a Pharisee among Pharisees. One could argue he was a career priest and politician.

As a high-standing Pharisee in the Sanhedrin, Nicodemus would have been required to come from a lineage of Pharisees. At the age of two, his father would have placed a written portion of the Torah dipped in honey on his tongue, creating an early memory associated with the sweetness of God's promises (Psalm 119:103). By age four, Nicodemus would have started memorizing Leviticus. By twelve, he would have committed Genesis through Deuteronomy to memory. And by fifteen, he would have been able to quote the Prophets and the Psalms without needing to glance at the scrolls. When he publicly declared his faith, Nicodemus would have pledged to take the *yoke of the Torah upon himself*, fully embracing God's laws as reflected in the Torah. He diligently observed the daily hours of prayer, fasted twice a week, and tithed on his all of his income and possessions.

This was a man devoted to God, recognized and esteemed among Pharisees for not simply fulfilling his obligations but excelling in them.

Yet here stands Nicodemus, meeting with Jesus under the cover of night. Being seen with Jesus openly would have raised questions about his status among the priestly classes. So, at the risk of his reputation, Nicodemus approaches Jesus clandestinely, seeking to learn from the One who has been causing a stir among the people. He begins the conversation by acknowledging, *We know that you are a teacher who has come from God.*

This is a significant moment that we often overlook. Nicodemus isn't speaking for himself alone; he uses the word "we" to indicate that he represents others. Nicodemus understands the weight of his words. As a Pharisee among Pharisees, he recognizes the power of his chosen words. Yet, here he is, meeting with this scandalous itinerant teacher who performs miracles and speaks with authority, and Nicodemus declares, *We know you are a teacher from God.*

Nicodemus bestows a high honor upon Jesus. It's not a sneer or a jab; it's not part of a public debate or an insidious accusation thrown at Jesus in a town square (as Jesus was accustomed to from the Pharisees). This is Nicodemus, a man who possesses an unparalleled knowledge of God's Word, acknowledging that something extraordinary is happening in his presence. He has drawn closer to the source of this mystery, even risking his lofty reputation by meeting Jesus under the cover of darkness.

And when Jesus tells Nicodemus that one must be born again to see the kingdom of God, this learned man, this career priest and politician who has studied the Word of God from his earliest memories, is utterly dumbfounded.

So of course, we've reduced this profound statement to a catchphrase that we throw on billboards and banners.

However, being born again is a mystery to be embraced, inviting a radical encounter of the supernatural and of the Heavens into our physical world. But before delving into the mystery of being born again, let's reflect on what we have done with Jesus' words.

As humans tend to do, we turned the idea of being born again into a saying. Taking it a step further, we transformed being born again into a ritual, something we do – *Okay, publicly declare in front of our church that you're a Christian, let's baptize you, and now you're part of 'our' tribe and born again. Please fill out our connect card and we will follow up with a call to get you involved in our church volunteer program!*

But is that what Jesus meant?

Far from it.

Let me be clear; this is not a criticism of the act of baptism. Baptism is a powerful and necessary step that we should take. It is a public declaration of our new identity in Christ, and we should embrace it. However, all too often, this "new identity" remains bound to a social construct, that of becoming a "good Christian," instead of fully embracing our identity as sons and daughters of God.

And being baptized in water is not the same as being born again.

Let me say that again. Being baptized is *not* being born again. Baptism is a public declaration of being born again.

But what does *born again* really mean?

All too often, we look at being "born again" as an *add-on* to our old self, and by just reducing it to a baptism ritual, we completely miss out. Yes, there is a need for water baptism. After all, one of my most powerful moments with God came after my own baptism, so I personally know how powerful of a moment it is. But the process of baptism is merely symbolic of something we all too often miss and ignore – that of actually being born again into the Kingdom of God and manifesting that Kingdom wherever we go and in whatever we put our hands to.

Quite simply, too many of us settle for being dunked in water and thinking that's the grand awesomeness of faith ... rather than being immersed continually in the living waters of Jesus and letting that flow from our hearts, minds, mouths, bellies, and into the world.

When Jesus says that we must be born again, He means that we must be born into who God created us to be – stepping into the reality of who we are in *His Spirit*. Our identities are no longer based on what the world says about us or the goals we've attained. Instead, as a child of God, who God created us to be always come *first*, and we move from there. We must be born again into who God created us to be.

And that is anything but an add-on.

Because, after being born again, we cannot just return to how we used to be.

A Case of Mistaken Identity Redux

Take the example of beautiful and mysterious Caerleon. Once it was revealed to be an ancient Roman fortress and amphitheater responsible for housing 30,000 Roman troops at a time, could it realistically be called the site of King Arthur's Round Table?

No.

Instead, Caerleon is now known as the place that people *once thought of* as the site of King Arthur's Table. But now the archaeological remnants on site are known by their true identity. Its true worth and glory has now been revealed and can't be covered up any longer. The overgrowth has been pulled away. The gold has been identified and revealed.

To reveal the Kingdom of God, to walk in it, to see it, you must be born again. You have to step into the reality of who God says you are.

You must excavate away the junk you thought was you and realize who you are – an empowered Son or Daughter who is loved and commissioned to reveal God's Glory to a world in desperate need of its revelation.

When you know His Spirit, when the real you is revealed, there is something that you instinctively know – you are royalty. You are the Son or Daughter of the King of the Universe. And royalty has a responsibility to reign righteously - to do justly, to love mercy, and to walk humbly with God (Micah 6:8).

Being born again into the Kingdom of God is realizing that God is not an add-on to the old way you did life. HE IS THE SOURCE. He is the cornerstone of what you build upon. Being *born again* into the Kingdom of God is knowing that YOU cannot go back to who you used to be.

And why would you want to?

Realizing Your True Worth

I know who you are.

Do you?

It doesn't matter if you live in a trailer down by the river or you live in a penthouse. When you know who you are in God, you are royalty. And you will begin to know the Kingdom and reveal Him wherever you go. You can't help it. That's what real children do. They bear the image of their parents. You do the work of the Kingdom because of who you are, not something that you are striving to be.

What is born of the flesh is of the world. It is the world that is the add-on, not the other way around. We can only step into who we truly are through His Spirit, the true source of what YOU are. And when that Spirit blows, you might find yourself like me, halfway across the world, reveling in the glory of the Lord on mission. Or, you may be in your hometown, radically shifting the atmosphere of your workplace just by being who you truly are – a child of God.

God's heart and the first step to intimacy with Him is to reveal your true identity in Christ so you can release His love and become like Him, moving from glory to glory. He desires to overwhelm your world with the reality of how HE sees you, and to revolutionize the way you see and even think about yourself, and about Him! God's no longer distant or far away. He is right here in you. And you, are with Him. You are never alone. You are never in need. You are filled to overflowing, and His grace and mercy radically pursue you all the days of your life, even when walking through the valley of the shadow of death.

When you embrace your true identity, you begin to step into the realization of who you are in Christ, and you will change the very fabric of reality of your earthly world. Your God-given nature begins to transform your earthly nature. And you become a light on a hill.

And all you have to do is ask – *Papa, you're a good, good Father. Show me who I am in your eyes.*

And don't let go until He begins to show you. Embrace it. And live from being *born again*.

But there's something very important to consider about being born again. It is messy. To the child, birth is violent - the pushing, the forced movement, the contractions, the pressure of being expelled from the comfortable and the compact into a sometimes frightening and wide-open brand-new world. But it is a world you were created for and designed to impact. And this world, this Kingdom, it is now yours. Perhaps this is the deeper mystery behind what Jesus said in Matthew 11:12, *the kingdom of heaven suffers violence, and the violent take it by force.*

Ask, and you shall receive, seek and you shall find, knock...and it will be given to you. Being born again into who you are is the only free gift that will cost you everything.

And being born again is just the beginning.

Close your eyes. Draw in a deep breath through your nose. Release it out through your mouth. Take another breath, realizing that the very breath in your lungs was created by an infinite being who created that very air, and created a world where that air has recirculated from time on Earth began. You are not just breathing in air, but you are breathing in atoms that have been in existence for billions of years. You are breathing in particles with memory from the most ancient of days, engineered by a

God who held you in his mind when He molded the first molecules of air that would one day flow in your lungs, giving you the kiss of life.

Now release the air in your lungs, not just expelling the false memory of you, but also releasing what it is that God is placing in you now – *new life*. In breathing out the carbon dioxide, you are feeding the plants and the trees. The teeming life of the earth is breathing in what you are releasing. You are part of this Earth, commissioned by your Father to responsibly pick up the mandate given in the Garden of Eden -to be fruitful, multiply, fill, gently subdue, and cultivate the Earth. You are to garden creation with the very breath in your lungs, releasing an awareness of the Glory of the Lord to everything around you.

It's as simple as breathing.

Let's Return To Original Design

We began this session with a question.

Who are you?

And I want you to look back at that sentence you wrote when we started this segment. And I want you to write it again.

But this time, I want you to write who you are.

—   ——   —   ———   —   ——

I   AM   A   CHILD   OF   GOD

Now breathe in deep. And bring the breath of life deep inside, tasting the air as a newborn child.

And when you're ready, child of God, it's time to take your first steps, right into the arms of your Father.

Scripture References

Genesis 1:28: "God blessed them, and God said to them, 'Be fruitful and multiply, and fill the earth and subdue it; and have dominion over the fish of the sea and over the birds of the air and over every living thing that moves upon the earth.'"

Genesis 2:7: "Then the Lord God formed man from the dust of the ground, and breathed into his nostrils the breath of life; and the man became a living being."

Genesis 2:15: "The Lord God took the man and put him in the garden of Eden to till it and keep it."

Jeremiah 1:5: "Before I formed you in the womb I knew you, and before you were born I consecrated you; I appointed you a prophet to the nations."

Psalm 100:3: "Know that the Lord is God. It is he that made us, and we are his; we are his people, and the sheep of his pasture."

Psalm 119:103: "How sweet are your words to my taste, sweeter than honey to my mouth!"

Psalm 119:105: "Your word is a lamp to my feet and a light to my path."

Psalm 139:13-16: "For it was you who formed my inward parts; you knit me together in my mother's womb. I praise you, for I am fearfully and wonderfully made. Wonderful are your works; that I know very well. My frame was not hidden from you, when I was being made in secret, intricately woven in the depths of the earth. Your eyes beheld my unformed substance. In your book were written all the days that were formed for me, when none of them as yet existed."

Matthew 7:7: "Ask, and it will be given you; search, and you will find; knock, and the door will be opened for you."

Matthew 11:12: "From the days of John the Baptist until now the kingdom of heaven suffers violence, and the violent take it by force."

Matthew 14:9: "Jesus said to him, 'Have I been with you all this time, Philip, and you still do not know me? Whoever has seen me has seen the Father. How can you say, 'Show us the Father'?'"

John 1:12-13: "But to all who received him, who believed in his name, he gave power to become children of God, who were born, not of blood or of the will of the flesh or of the will of man, but of God."

John 3:3-8: "Jesus answered him, 'Very truly, I tell you, no one can see the kingdom of God without being born from above.' Nicodemus said to him, 'How can anyone be born after having grown old? Can one enter a second time into the mother's womb and be born?' Jesus answered,

'Very truly, I tell you, no one can enter the kingdom of God without being born of water and Spirit. What is born of the flesh is flesh, and what is born of the Spirit is spirit. Do not be astonished that I said to you, 'You must be born from above.' The wind blows where it chooses, and you hear the sound of it, but you do not know where it comes from or where it goes. So it is with everyone who is born of the Spirit.'"

Romans 8:15: "For you did not receive a spirit of slavery to fall back into fear, but you have received a spirit of adoption. When we cry, 'Abba! Father!'"

Romans 8:16: "It is that very Spirit bearing witness with our spirit that we are children of God."

Romans 8:29: "For those whom he foreknew he also predestined to be conformed to the image of his Son, in order that he might be the firstborn within a large family."

Ephesians 1:3-6: "Blessed be the God and Father of our Lord Jesus Christ, who has blessed us in Christ with every spiritual blessing in the heavenly places, just as he chose us in Christ before the foundation of the world to be holy and blameless before him in love. He destined us for adoption as his children through Jesus Christ, according to the good pleasure of his will, to the praise of his glorious grace that he freely bestowed on us in the Beloved."

Ephesians 2:10: "For we are what he has made us, created in Christ Jesus for good works, which God prepared beforehand to be our way of life."

1 Peter 1:3: "Blessed be the God and Father of our Lord Jesus Christ! By his great mercy he has given us a new birth into a living hope through the resurrection of Jesus Christ from the dead."

1 John 3:1: "See what love the Father has given us, that we should be called children of God; and that is what we are."

2 Corinthians 5:17: "So if anyone is in Christ, there is a new creation: everything old has passed away; see, everything has become new!"

Galatians 2:20: "I have been crucified with Christ; and it is no longer I who live, but it is Christ who lives in me. And the life I now live in the flesh I live by faith in the Son of God, who loved me and gave himself for me."

Titus 3:5: "He saved us, not because of any works of righteousness that we had done, but according to his mercy, through the water of rebirth and renewal by the Holy Spirit."

Notes

Initial

_____

_____

_____

_____

_____

_____

_____

_____

_____

_____

_____

_____

_____

Later

_____

_____

_____

_____

_____

REVELATION TWO

SEEING YOUR FATHER FOR WHO HE IS

H ello there, world changer. How do you feel? I hope the air tastes a bit different. Maybe more alive, perhaps? Enjoy this space. Don't rush past it.

Waking up to a new reality isn't always easy. For a long while, you will find that it is a continual process of renewal. Thoughts will want to intrude and bring you back to where you used to be. But when those thoughts begin to intrude, you must realize something very important.

You must realize that *THAT* person is gone.

Do you not know that all of us who were baptized into Christ Jesus were baptized into his death? Therefore, we were buried with him by baptism into death, so that, just as Christ was raised from the dead by the glory of the Father, so we also might walk in newness of life. – Romans 6:3-5

Remember, those intrusive thoughts aren't the born-again you. They are from the old you. And when they rise in you, when the thoughts of the old you begin whispering in the recesses of your memory, not only are you to take every thought captive (2 Corinthians 10:5) but you are to *repent*.

Now when I say repent that doesn't mean groveling on your face or putting on sackcloth and lamenting loudly in the streets how you've done horrible things. I mean to turn your heart and mind back to who God says you are, who you are in your born-again existence, and renew your mind in this revelation - *Do not conform to the pattern of this world, but be transformed by the renewing of your mind* -Romans 12:2.

And now that you are just beginning to see who you really are, it's time to explore another important question.

How do you describe God?

Ask an average person what they believe the Christian God to be like, and chances are, several answers will pop up. And when you specifically ask *a non-Christian* what the Christian God is like, well, the results aren't pretty. Even a furtive glance across social media channels, television, and interviews from the general public reveals that for the average non-believer the Christian God is often described as angry, mad, silent, disappointed, wrathful, indifferent, or absent.

And don't forget, pretty dang *judge-y.*

What else should we expect, though? Especially when 48% of American Christians believe that upon God's orders, Jesus will return with blood dripping from His robe and a sword emanating from his mouth and bringing wholesale slaughter with Him to anyone that doesn't believe or think as they do.

That is some scary stuff. Especially when taken out of historic context (and we'll come back to that in a video session later).

But we have to admit that the non-Christian view of Yahweh is rather poor. And the views of God as angry and retributive, indifferent, and judgmental are common.

But what if I told you that God was none of those things?

What if I told you that the truth of who God IS has been stolen from you, and the image you have been left with is a lie - forged in an attempt to separate you from not just knowing who YOU are ... but WHOSE you are?

As you are now understanding what it actually means to be born again, it's time to wipe the gunk from your eyes and mind. For in the womb, you heard your Father's voice. And it's time to see Him with your own eyes.

The Case of CONTINUED Mistaken Identity

While living in the UK for five years, one of my favorite areas to explore was a scant few miles away from our cottage, an archeological wonder called Margam Park. Margam is a breathtaking location filled with picturesque landscapes, expansive gardens, monastery ruins, and a castle that is still open for special events. The lands of Margam have a spiritual history that dates back over 5,000 years. And once considered holy ground by the Silures, a Celtic tribe of dark-skinned curly-haired warriors, in the 11th century, a Norman Marcher Lord, the infamous Robert Fitzhamon, claimed the lands of Margam for his own.

Now, if you're not a big fan of history, don't roll your eyes and close this book. I promise this is the last time we will do a Welsh history deep dive (maybe). But this bit of history holds a powerful parallel to the subject at hand and will draw something ugly out into the open so that we can tackle it head-on.

The invasion of the Marcher Lords from England into Wales began a centuries-long bloody chapter in the history of Britain. Desiring new territory and resources, the King of England set his sights west towards the rugged frontier, a country known today as Wales. And to accomplish his goals, the king assigned men of a certain character to the task - men known for their cunning, ruthlessness, thirst for power, and bloodlust.

Robert Fitzhamon

And few, if any Marcher Lords, were as feared as Robert FitzHamon. Marcher Lords were a law unto themselves, and FitzHamon cut a bloody path throughout South Wales in 1091 AD, seizing territory, and murdering every Welsh prince who stood in his way. He was merciless, even going so far as to demand one mile of gold coins from one prince as tribute, a tribute *which he actually received*.

FitzHamon and his Twelve Knights of Glamorgan built castles across South Wales to institute control, and many of these castles remain today, echoes of the Marcher Lords' bloody domination.

When Robert FitzHamon died in 1107, all of his Welsh holdings passed to his daughter, Mabel. And Mabel married Robert, 1st Earl of Gloucester, the son of King Henry of England. This strategic marriage consolidated the Welsh lands FitzHamon took by force with that of royal English blood, creating a blood claim to Welsh land, making Mabel and Robert the region's power couple. And like Fitzhamon, Robert and Mabel continued to acquire Welsh territory, lands, and wealth through bloody and brutal campaigns of subjugation and political conniving.

The powerful union of Robert, Earl of Gloucester & Countess Mabel Fitzhamon

But strangely, after a bout with serious illness in 1147 AD, Robert Earl of Gloucester granted 18,000 acres of prime real estate to an abbot named William Clairvaux to build an abbey and monastery dedicated to the Blessed Virgin Mary - right smack dab on the lands that he had seized by the blood of the Welsh, and directly on the site of a Celtic Christian monastery that had existed there since 600 AD.

And two months after signing his lands to Clairvaux, Robert was dead.

And with the granting of 18,000 acres to the *extremely* wealthy Cistercian monks of Clairvaux, Wales' spiritual history would be forever changed. Wales was going to leave the simplicity of Celtic Christianity behind and instead get a taste of the *"big time"* Christianity that was popular upon the European continent.

Immediately, work began on a building project the size of which had *never been seen in Wales before* - for FORTY YEARS skilled craftsmen worked around the clock - shaping stone to build an abbey, church, cloister, and offices befitting an esteemed daughter house of St Bernard's Cistercian House of Clairvaux, Normandy. By the end of the 12th century, Margam Abbey was the most powerful monastery in Western Britain. And the abbey and its monks were central to the social, cultural, and religious life of South Wales.

The ruins of Margam today

The remains of their work still exist today. And they are truly stunning, creating an otherworldly atmosphere like something out of a dream. The grounds are open to the public and consist of the monastery ruins, the church and cloister, and even a castle erected centuries later from the ruined stones. They are fantastic ruins to explore, and Margam's wonders are even used for movie sets when CGI isn't going to do the trick.

But let's dial back and address an underlying question most do not think to ask when learning of this place.

Why would a Marcher Lord, responsible for the brutal subjugation of the Welsh people and who had never shown a tendency towards real piety, grant 18,000 acres of primo real estate to a Christian monastery upon his deathbed?

The answer isn't pretty.

During the Middle Ages, it was common practice for lords and landowners to give large portions of their land to the Roman Catholic Church. It was believed that in doing so, they could ensure salvation not just for themselves, but in some cases, their descendants. And the Church would, in turn, guarantee salvation through a contract, called a charter, which in exchange for lands, livestock, and gifts, would fireproof the souls of the soon-to-be deceased.

A medieval charter

So feudal lords, who may have felt a bit responsible for atrocities and the spilled blood that occurred during their time on Earth (especially during campaigns as brutal as those of the Marcher Lords in Wales), gave large portions of their lands to the Church as a "get out of hell free" card when death was drawing near.

And this was not a rare practice, nor was it considered strange. This was a common method of ensuring one's salvation, with lords, ladies, and property-holders handing over grand swathes of lands and fortunes to the Church. Medieval man was terrified of God's judgment and wraith, and, let's face it - when you know your time is coming, wouldn't you do whatever you could to avoid eternal damnation?

So, if you could secure salvation by donating land or performing works, why wouldn't you try?

Anything to stay away from hellfire, right?

Now you may chuckle at this. Or you might even get a bit angry. But here's the thing. Put a lid on your anger or disgust. Because most of us, whether we know it or not, still operate under this MESSED UP system.

The Truth Shall Set You Free

Here's the thing. On the surface, most of us understand that we can't buy salvation. And we know we can't buy off God's "anger" with land, donations, or property. But in truth, most of us only understand this *on the surface*. Because reality shows us that subconsciously, we think otherwise.

In our religious systems, how often do we try to buy off God's anger with our good works? How often do you *do the right thing* to try to gain God's favor?

How often do we *act* a certain way because of what we get, say ... a blessing like salvation? Or a blessing in our health? How about when we give or tithe because we've been told if we do so, then we receive a financial blessing in return?

Ah. Now you're getting it.

At its heart, this is simple manipulation. It's transactional. And you know what they say about manipulation – it's the spirit of witchcraft.

And it's amazing how many Christians resort to witchcraft to get what they want, instead of moving from an intimate relationship with a Father who loves His children and GIVES great gifts.

You see, when we attempt to buy God off and when our relationship with Him is based on transactions, it reveals our poor fundamental misunderstanding of who God is. And it reveals that *the truth of who your Father is has been stolen from you*.

Because … God isn't angry. And you don't have to bribe Him.

And understanding this is a MASSIVE lesson in your journey of discovering intimacy with God.

God is in love with you.

He created you to spend eternity with you, to enjoy you as a good Father does His children. And He fully intends to see this come to pass.

You can't buy what is a free gift - God's love, His healing, His salvation, and His deliverance.

It's a gift from a Father who loves His children, a Father who is *Love Himself* according to 1 John 4:8. And according to 2 Peter 3:9, it's the Father's desire that none of His children perish.

God desires a relationship with you, and we have such a poor understanding of ourselves as His children because the world has a poor understanding of God. And that's 1 John 3:1, by the way.

To understand WHO we are, we have to understand WHOSE we are. We have to see God for who He truly is.

So much of our artwork, images, and beliefs about God are just plain wrong. God's not a terrifying Zeus-like figure in the clouds who has this gigantic list of things we've done wrong, just chomping at the bit to send us to a fiery abyss.

He's not angry at you, disappointed in you, or holding your mistakes above your head. God said *I, yes I, am He who blots out your transgressions for My own sake and remembers your sins no more* in Isaiah 43:25. And Hebrews 8:12 says *And I will forgive their wickedness, and I will never again remember their sins.*

You see, just like the lands of Wales were stolen away by the brutal Marcher Lords, much of our understanding about the truth of who God is has been stolen away by the dark specter of religion.

We are taught to fear God because of our perceived failures and to hide away from Him, and then we're taught that we're supposed to try and buy Him off with our good works.

But that's not who He is *OR* what He desires.

Yes, God is a God of justice and righteousness, and He is holy. And God certainly doesn't care much for sin. But Moses described God as *the compassionate and gracious God, slow to anger, abounding in love and faithfulness, maintaining love to thousands, and forgiving wickedness, rebellion, and sin* in Exodus 34:5-7.

And that was Moses' poor and limited *purely human* understanding of God.

But Jesus, who knows a bit more about God than any other being in existence, described God differently.

Jesus called God something that a first-century Jew would have thought of as absolutely revolutionary. Jesus called God *Father*

Seeing God as God Truly Is

Before Jesus, God was not referred to as an intimate Father. Sure, to a first-century Jew, God was *titled* the father and protector of the poor, the orphan, and the widow. God was the lawgiver and the helper and judge of Israel. And Isaiah 63 reflects on God as a father of the world concerning creation, and His covenant role as father of Israel, his chosen people.

But for the first-century Hebraic mindset, God's title as Father was simply a metaphor.

Just like it is for most of us today.

But Jesus referred to God as a Father in the literal sense.

And Jesus showed that God wasn't a distant Father who was angry with His kids like everyone thought. He was a Father who was passionate and desired an active relationship with his children.

Jesus said that God was not far away, nor was he withholding. God was actively seeking His children like a shepherd does his sheep, calling them to Him, calling them home to His Kingdom that He was establishing on earth through His Son.

Jesus revealed that God doesn't set up barriers between himself and his children. God demolished and ripped up barriers with the arrival, sacrifice, and resurrection of Jesus, his Beloved. And Jesus proclaimed something even more radical - that when we believed in Him, saw Him for who He was, and believed in what He did for us with His sacrifice and resurrection, we gained the right to be called children of God because we now have access to the Father through Him in John 1:12-13!

But watch out, because here is where false belief tries to sneak back in. This is where the nasty religious spirit typically creeps up, begins to twist and manipulate, and says something akin to *Well, even if all of that is true, then that means Jesus is the reason God loves you.*

But that's not the truth. Not even close.

That's an intrusive thief trying to steal the truth from you.

The truth is that Jesus came to show *us* how much God loves *us*. Jesus came to show you the truth about your Father.

For God so loved the world that HE sent his only begotten Son.

You must see God for who He is – a Father radically in love with you.

What the Father Wants for You

Because of the Father's love and Jesus' love, you have the freedom of the Kingdom of God, a revelation of a new identity as a son and daughter, bringing an end to the worldly and religious idea of separation from God. God is not distant. Father is not far away. God was, and is today, restoring to His children the truth of their birthright.

And this love is not something you can earn.

It's a gift.

And now, because of our re-establishment as children of God, we do the work of God's Kingdom because it is our family business. We don't do works, donate lands, and build monasteries to achieve salvation. We don't have to attempt to buy God off with gifts and titles. And we don't have to suck up to Him to receive His favor.

Now we do the works of God's Kingdom because these works are a natural overflow of our hearts and identities. We do the work of the Kingdom, and we give of ourselves because of what we are – God's children.

It's not hard work. It's not drudgery. It's not something to check off on some "discipleship chart." When you truly come alive because of Jesus and have faith in the reality of what He has done, the work of the Kingdom becomes an overflow of your renewed heart and mind.

This understanding of God and His desired relationship with us was a complete paradigm shift for the first-century Jew - and in truth, it's much the same for us 2,000 years later!

And when you know WHOSE you are, when you see God for who he is and his overabundant love for you, you can *begin* to become WHO you are. When you see God for who He truly is – the Father who loves His children - everything changes.

And what was stolen, becomes reclaimed.

The Absolute Truth About Your Salvation

God doesn't care how much land you give, how many orphanages you build, how many charities you start, how many folks you lead to Him, or how much money you give to the Church. If God doesn't have your heart, if you don't know Him and your foundation isn't in Him, your works will be considered as wood, hay, and stubble and will burn away. Now, when this is mentioned in 1 Corinthians 3:15 Paul makes sure to say that *if the work is burned up, the builder will suffer loss;* but Paul adds *the builder will be saved, but only as through fire.*

God is not interested in your works as much as He is interested in your desire to know him.

God wants you to see Him as He is. He wants you to see His goodness and love as reflected in Jesus.

And his mercy.

And that mercy doesn't just extend to the world at large. It extends to you.

Because God knows if you see his love and receive it, that is where you will find your salvation. For when we see Jesus, we see God. After all, in John 14:9 Jesus even said *Whoever has seen Me has seen the Father.*

Salvation can't be earned through your works, efforts, or donations. It's a gift. When we read the word *salvation* in the Bible, that word in Greek is SOZO, which means a complete package of salvation, deliverance, and healing. Salvation isn't a magic prayer and a *get-out-of-hell-free* card, as we often treat it, and has been sold to us by snake oil salesmen and swindlers looking for your *"seed money."* SOZO is healing from the inside out of the soul, an infilling of the Spirit, a washing away of the old, and the cool refreshment of becoming a new *kainos-created* being.

Cast your mind back to what we covered in Revelation 1. You are not the old you. You have been born again. And 2 Corinthians 5:17 flatly states that *if anyone is in Christ, there is a new creation: everything old has passed away; see, everything has become new!* And the word for creation in the original koine Greek is *kainos*, meaning *new in kind and in contrast to what previously existed, so taking the place thereof.*

Salvation is stepping into and transforming us into our true reality, that of a Child of God. And this is a gift given to us by a loving God who made US in HIS image – creative beings who have it within us to sculpt a world with His glory, according to Gen 1:28.

Your Father Revealed

It's time to shatter the religious paradigms and pull apart the chains placed upon you.

You don't need to buy or work your way into God's favor. The truth is that you already exist in it.

You don't need to earn God's love. Because you already have it.

And when you understand that, when you accept that deep inside, and when that mustard seed starts to sprout in your heart, *all of a sudden, what changes is your ability to see and receive your Father's love for you.*

Jesus didn't come to change God's mind about the world. Jesus came to change the world's mind, and God's Children's minds, about their Father *because he FIRST loved us* (1 John 4:19).

And it's time for you to reclaim what was stolen.

It's time for you to take the next step of moving into real intimacy with your Father.

It's time for you to see your Father for who He is.

So, what's stopping you?

Let's do it right now.

I want you to close your eyes. And once again, take a deep breath. And again, while breathing in, I want you to visualize pulling in the air created on Earth from the beginning of time, the atoms, the particles, the history of the Earth, and the memory of all that has been created. The very first breath that God put into Adam's lungs is still the same air you breathe today.

Holding this breath in your lungs, I want you to imagine the endless love of God for you. If you can't physically feel it yet, that's okay. But visualize a river flowing towards you. And that's all I want you to imagine. A river. If more comes to you, that's fine. If you see a throne, rainbow, or whatever else comes into your mind, that's fine. But I want you to focus on the river right now. If you would like to step into it, then step. If you want to sit on the bank and watch it go by, that is also okay.

As you release your breath, take a moment to feel the movement of the Earth under your feet. And turning your attention away from the river, visualize the span of swirling galaxies, the brilliant stars, the revolving planets, all of creation, and realize that yes, God created those wonderful things to shine ...

But He created YOU to love.

And as you keep breathing, just for a few moments, continue to breathe in the air that God placed into Adam's lungs, the air that holds the history of the world. As you hold your breath, visualize the flowing river. And when you release, feel the Earth, and see swirling galaxies, all things moving in a symphony of motion. And do all of this knowing that it was YOU he created to have a relationship with.

Feel His glory all around you. Because His glory fills the earth as the water covers the sea. His Glory is everywhere.

What has been lacking is your awareness of it.

So breathe. And breathe in the reality of Him, and who He is.

And when you begin to grasp the truth of God's reality and how he feels about you, then you can see the tears in the veil of separation. You can see the threads torn asunder from the inside out and billowing in the warm breeze. Feel the wind against your cheek as you peer into the beyond.

I implore you to take time with this. Please don't go rushing on to the next chapter just to complete the book. Park here for a bit. Resonate here for a moment. This is a special moment I don't want you to miss.

The Father loves you. He has always loved you. You were created to look upon His face. You are a kainos creation, and the old has passed away.

What do you see beyond the torn veil? What do you hear?

Do you hear the sound of far-off bells, ringing in celebration?

Are the bells drawing near? Or are you drawing nearer to the bells?

Listen to them, the sound of bells drifting ever closer.

For the bells toll for you.

Scripture References

Genesis 1:28 - "God blessed them, and God said to them, 'Be fruitful and multiply, and fill the earth and subdue it; and have dominion over the fish of the sea and over the birds of the air and over every living thing that moves upon the earth.'"

Jeremiah 1:5 - "Before I formed you in the womb I knew you, and before you were born I consecrated you; I appointed you a prophet to the nations."

Psalm 100:3 - "Know that the Lord is God. It is he that made us, and we are his; we are his people, and the sheep of his pasture."

Psalm 139:13-16 - "For it was you who formed my inward parts; you knit me together in my mother's womb. I praise you, for I am fearfully and wonderfully made. Wonderful are your works; that I know very well. My frame was not hidden from you, when I was being made in secret, intricately woven in the depths of the earth. Your eyes beheld my unformed substance. In your book were written all the days that were formed for me, when none of them as yet existed."

John 1:12-13 - "But to all who received him, who believed in his name, he gave power to become children of God, who were born, not of blood or of the will of the flesh or of the will of man, but of God."

John 3:3-8 - "Jesus answered him, 'Very truly, I tell you, no one can see the kingdom of God without being born from above.' Nicodemus said to him, 'How can anyone be born after having grown old? Can one enter a second time into the mother's womb and be born?' Jesus answered, 'Very truly, I tell you, no one can enter the kingdom of God without being born of water and Spirit. What is born of the flesh is flesh, and what is born of the Spirit is spirit. Do not be astonished that I said to you, "You must be born from above." The wind blows where it chooses, and you hear the sound of it, but you do not know where it comes from or where it goes. So it is with everyone who is born of the Spirit.'"

Romans 6:3-5 - "Do you not know that all of us who have been baptized into Christ Jesus were baptized into his death? Therefore we have been buried with him by baptism into death, so that, just as Christ was raised from the dead by the glory of the Father, so we too might walk in newness of life. For if we have been united with him in a death like his, we will certainly be united with him in a resurrection like his."

2 Corinthians 10:5 - "We destroy arguments and every proud obstacle raised up against the knowledge of God, and we take every thought captive to obey Christ."

Romans 12:2 - "Do not be conformed to this world, but be transformed by the renewing of your minds, so that you may discern what is the will of God—what is good and acceptable and perfect."

Ephesians 1:4-6 - "Just as he chose us in Christ before the foundation of the world to be holy and blameless before him in love. He destined us for adoption as his children through Jesus Christ, according to the good pleasure of his will, to the praise of his glorious grace that he freely bestowed on us in the Beloved."

Ephesians 2:10 - "For we are what he has made us, created in Christ Jesus for good works, which God prepared beforehand to be our way of life."

Titus 3:5 - "He saved us, not because of any works of righteousness that we had done, but according to his mercy, through the water of rebirth and renewal by the Holy Spirit."

2 Timothy 1:9 - "who saved us and called us with a holy calling, not according to our works but according to his own purpose and grace. This grace was given to us in Christ Jesus before the ages began."

John 14:9 - "Jesus said to him, 'Have I been with you all this time, Philip, and you still do not know me? Whoever has seen me has seen the Father. How can you say, "Show us the Father"?'

Galatians 2:20 - "and it is no longer I who live, but it is Christ who lives in me. And the life I now live in the flesh I live by faith in the Son of God, who loved me and gave himself for me."

1 Peter 1:3 - "Blessed be the God and Father of our Lord Jesus Christ! By his great mercy he has given us a new birth into a living hope through the resurrection of Jesus Christ from the dead."

Romans 8:15 - "For you did not receive a spirit of slavery to fall back into fear, but you have received a spirit of adoption. When we cry, 'Abba! Father!'"

Isaiah 43:25 - "I, I am He who blots out your transgressions for my own sake, and I will not remember your sins."

Exodus 34:5-6 - "The Lord descended in the cloud and stood with him there, and proclaimed the name, 'The Lord.' The Lord passed before him, and proclaimed, 'The Lord, the Lord, a God merciful and gracious, slow to anger, and abounding in steadfast love and faithfulness."

Psalm 103:13 - "As a father has compassion for his children, so the Lord has compassion for those who fear him."

Matthew 7:11 - "If you then, who are evil, know how to give good gifts to your children, how much more will your Father in heaven give good things to those who ask him!"

John 14:6 - "Jesus said to him, 'I am the way, and the truth, and the life. No one comes to the Father except through me.'"

1 John 4:8 - "Whoever does not love does not know God, for God is love."

2 Peter 3:9 - "The Lord is not slow about his promise, as some think of slowness, but is patient with you, not wanting any to perish, but all to come to repentance."

Hebrews 8:12 - "For I will be merciful toward their iniquities, and I will remember their sins no more."

Luke 15:4-7 - "Which one of you, having a hundred sheep and losing one of them, does not leave the ninety-nine in the wilderness and go after the one that is lost until he finds it? When he has found it, he lays it on his shoulders and rejoices. And when he comes home, he calls together his friends and neighbors, saying to them, 'Rejoice with me, for I have found my sheep that was lost.' Just so, I tell you, there will be more joy in heaven over one sinner who repents than over ninety-nine righteous persons who need no repentance."

Galatians 4:6 - "And because you are children, God has sent the Spirit of his Son into our hearts, crying, 'Abba! Father!'"

Ephesians 3:14-15 - "For this reason I bow my knees before the Father, from whom every family in heaven and on earth takes its name."

John 3:16 - "For God so loved the world that he gave his only Son, so that everyone who believes in him may not perish but may have eternal life."

Romans 5:8 - "But God proves his love for us in that while we still were sinners Christ died for us."

1 John 4:19 - "We love because he first loved us."

Ephesians 2:8-9 - "For by grace you have been saved through faith, and this is not your own doing; it is the gift of God—not the result of works, so that no one may boast."

Acts 17:28 - "For 'In him we live and move and have our being'; as even some of your own poets have said, 'For we too are his offspring.'"

Ephesians 1:18 - "I pray that the eyes of your heart may be enlightened, so that you may know what is the hope to which he has called you, what are the riches of his glorious inheritance among the saints."

Ephesians 3:16-19 - "I pray that, according to the riches of his glory, he may grant that you may be strengthened in your inner being with power through his Spirit, and that Christ may dwell in your hearts through faith, as you are being rooted and grounded in love. I pray that you may have the power to comprehend, with all the saints, what is the breadth and length and height and depth, and to know the love of Christ that surpasses knowledge, so that you may be filled with all the fullness of God."

1 Corinthians 3:15 - "If the work is burned up, the builder will suffer loss; the builder will be saved, but only as through fire."

2 Corinthians 5:17 - "So if anyone is in Christ, there is a new creation: everything old has passed away; see, everything has become new!"

1 John 3:1-2 - "See what love the Father has given us, that we should be called children of God; and that is what we are. The reason the world does not know us is that it did not know him. Beloved, we are God's children now; what we will be has not yet been revealed. What we do know is this: when he is revealed, we will be like him, for we will see him as he is."

Notes

Initial
_____
_____
_____
_____
_____
_____
_____
_____
_____
_____
_____
_____
_____

Later
_____
_____
_____
_____
_____

REVELATION THREE

THE WEDDING INVITATION

In the heart of a green meadow, bathed in the gentle, golden hues of a setting sun, the perfect wedding unfolds like a tenderly composed symphony. It is a day where love itself seems to take a deep breath, pause, and smile, a moment where two souls intertwine in a timeless dance.

As guests arrive, they are embraced by the melodies of the soft breeze rustling through the majestic trees, whispering tales of everlasting life and devotion. The air is perfumed with the sweet scent of wildflowers and the promise of new beginnings. The world seems to slow its spin for just a moment, suspended in time by the allure of a day drenched in love.

An elegant archway, adorned with blooming roses and cascading ivy, serves as a hallowed sanctuary. And standing beneath it, a couple stands, their eyes gleaming with shared dreams and unspoken promises. Their hands are linked, each a comforting anchor for the other, as they prepare to voyage into the vast ocean of life together.

The bride, a vision of grace, is cloaked in a gown of iridescent silk, which shimmers and flows like starlight. She clutches a bouquet of delicate peonies, their soft blush matching the color of her cheeks. The groom, equally striking, is the epitome of quiet strength in his tailored suit, his face radiating an undeniable warmth, a beacon of his undying love.

As their vows resonate through the peaceful meadow, each word is a testament to their enduring bond. The echoes of their promises blend with the evening's lullaby, as the sun dips lower, painting the sky with the hues of their love – warm oranges, passionate purples, and soft pinks.

When they seal their vows with a tender kiss, the world seems to sigh in unison with them, celebrating the union of two hearts. The jubilant chime of bells rings out, echoing the symphony of their joy. Guests cheer, toasting to the couple's happiness, their laughter a melody that mingles with the rustling leaves and chirping birds, creating an orchestra of love and joy.

The perfect wedding is a testament to love's enduring promise, a day where two souls pledge to journey together, no matter where the path of life leads. It's a celebration that transcends the boundaries of time, a moment that's both an end and a beginning – the end of two separate journeys and the start of a shared adventure. And as the sun finally dips below the horizon, the newlywed's dance beneath the star-strewn sky, their love as limitless and enduring as the universe itself.

And now, let's step away from this sacred scene. But just for a moment. The wedding ceremony is a holy moment in nearly every religion and every culture. It is a transcendent moment that crosses the boundaries of time and space, symbolic of the unification of souls, thoughts, minds, and bodies. It is emblematic of intimacy, of two joining together in every way, two hearts becoming one.

But as I steal your attention away from this imaginary couple's perfect day, I must ask you a question.

Did you know that there is a very real wedding invitation with your name on it?

All that is waiting is your response.

But before you respond, here's the thing. This is going to be the greatest wedding that the universe has ever seen. And you're not going to be attending the wedding as a spectator.

It's a wedding between Jesus and His Bride, which is the Church.

Now when I say the Church, I don't mean the buildings and the institution. Those things are destined for decay and dust. When I say Church I'm talking about the collective, the ecclesia, *the called-out ones,* those that know His voice. It is God's people that make up the Church, and together, we are the bride.

But in this mystery, according to Jesus in Matthew 25, you are also being called as an individual to be prepared to walk that aisle.

So that means it's not just about the collective.

It's about *you.*

And it's not an imaginary scene. It is a very real wedding. And you are the one who will be walking the aisle.

That's right. You are the blushing bride. And it doesn't matter if you are male or female. *Because in Christ there is neither Jew nor Greek, there is neither slave nor free, there is neither male nor female; for you are all one in Christ Jesus* (Galatians 3:28).

And Jesus? Jesus is the groom. And He is waiting for you to walk the aisle and accept His outstretched hand.

Jesus as the Bridegroom

Jesus as the bridegroom. Sure, that SOUNDS good. But c'mon, what does that mean? Let's move past the head knowledge and seat this into your heart. Because it's important. And if you don't start getting this, your journey beyond the veil and into deeper intimacy will never be what it could be.

Think about it- Jesus as the groom, and YOU as the Bride.

Knowing Jesus as a groom?

Jesus as a husband?

This is a radical shift for many people. It's one thing to know Jesus as a savior and someone we're supposed to pray to and serve. And I'm not saying those things are wrong. They are beautiful understandings of Jesus.

But Jesus invites us to know Him deeper.

We're invited to know Jesus as a bride knows the husband.

And it doesn't get more intimate than that, does it?

This is not the picture of Jesus we're used to. Religion has twisted our perception of Jesus, thinking that His love is something that must be earned and that we are being graded on how hard we work and sacrifice. We're used to seeing Jesus hanging on a crucifix or made to feel like we must suffer in guilt and shame for what we caused Him to endure on the cross. Or worse, we live in fear of His angry judgment, waiting for Him to return and slaughter those who don't believe in Him.

But does this sound like the love of an adoring Bridegroom?

Can you earn real love? Is Jesus grading you out and keeping a list of what you're doing wrong and right? Is Jesus still hanging on the cross? And is He waiting to marry you just so He can punish you?

Let's strip this thing down and hold it up to the light.

Does that sound like a good marriage to you?

And please tell me you said NO to that question.

Let's put it in these terms. Does your significant other make you work for their love, force you into submission, use guilt to get their way, shame your decisions, or threaten you with their wraith? Does that sound like a loving partner? Does that sound like a relationship you would want to be a part of?

Let's be honest. It doesn't. I'd run as far as I could from a relationship like that.

And that's not what Jesus has for us.

But this brings up a disturbing question. Think of how relationship with Jesus has been presented to you in religious settings. Think of the guilt, shame, and condemnation most of us have accepted as part of the norm in our relationship with Christ. *What if most people walking the planet who say they love Jesus have no idea of what Jesus' love is?*

That's a frightening thought. Most of us have love and fear so intertwined that we don't know what pure, unfiltered love is! But John wrote:

> There is no fear in love, but perfect love drives out fear, because fear involves punishment. The one who fears has not been perfected in love. We love because He first loved us -1 John 4:18-19

So, let's talk about something we think we know a lot about, but actually don't.

Let's discuss God's love, which is Jesus' love.

The love a Groom has for His bride.

The Meaning of Love

A major concept we must grasp on our journey into intimacy with Christ is that our modern English translations of ancient Hebrew, Aramaic, and Greek - the original languages of the Bible - are lacking in their ability to carry the full weight of what the original writers of the text intended.

And this includes the word LOVE.

In the English language, we have one word for love.

Close your eyes right now and say it out loud - *LOVE.*

Now, sit on that word for a bit. Ruminate on it for a second.

L-O-V-E.

Love.

It's a powerful word, isn't it?

By saying the word LOVE out loud, you imagined a whole host of ideas, memories, and concepts as to what the word LOVE means to you. You may have thought back to an embrace, a kiss, a hug, or maybe special holidays with the family. You could have thought about loss, betrayal, or a hurt that has lodged down deep.

Love is a mighty word, and it is a formidable force.

Yet in Scripture, there are FIVE words that are defined as love - one Hebrew, four Greek - each carrying a different connotation and specific meaning in the context in which it is used.

- **ahava**   - a Hebrew word that describes emotionally in-tense bonds and covenantal relationships (examples are Genesis 24:67, Deuteronomy 4:37, Song of Songs 1:3)

- **agapao** - a Greek word, primarily used as a verb – to love; meaning preferential and unconditional love, usually presented as of God Himself, which isn't based upon the goodness of the person who receives it or in response to what they have done (John 3:16). **This is the love God has for His children**. Conversely, mankind can have agapao for God, but also has agapao for sin and darkness (John 3:19, 2 Peter 2:15)

- **agape** - similar to agapao (and sometimes mistranslated as agapao), agape is love between people, love of people for God, and God's love for humanity as a whole. **Agape love is rooted in deep appreciation and esteem of others and is the love that God requires of His people** (John 15:12-13))

- **phileo** - is a Greek word that expresses *the feeling* of love; friendship, affection, and personal attachment. It's also the word for kiss. **Phileo is not commanded as agape is, especially regarding God and other people. Feelings can't be commanded, they must be a natural flow from the heart** (John 21))

- **philadelphia** is the loving of someone as a brother or sister, the love that members of the Church body are supposed to have for one another (Romans 12:10, Hebrews 13:1)

Now, these examples are the ones just found in the Bible. In ancient Greece *nine* words represented different forms of love (eros, phileo, ludus, storge, philautia, pragma, agape, agapao, philadelphia). All words and concepts English speakers attempt to group under one term – love.

The Truth Behind the Bridegroom's Love

At this point, you might be asking why understanding the various meanings of the word LOVE is a big deal.

Well, it's not a big deal. IT IS *THE* DEAL.

When you understand that when John wrote *"for God so loved the world"* in John 3:16 and he used the word *agapao*, you realize that John wasn't just using the word "love" to imply a feeling ... you know, like we humans do.

John was saying God's love was unconditional towards the object of his affection; a constant, perfect love not based upon a whim; a love that sought after the best for all, even when the subjects of His love did nothing to deserve His love. It's not a love that can be taken away or a love based on what we've done. It's a love that begins with Him and ends with Him and is to be received freely.

You cannot earn it.

And it never goes away.

What changes is that when we begin to even partially understand this agapao love, in as much as we could ever understand something so divinely miraculous, we can then begin to be able to receive and partake of that love.

In fact, when John used the word agapao in the context of 1 John 4:8, it translates as a love feast! God's love for us is like a yummy, luscious wedding feast, where all the most desirous pleasures of the universe are placed on an endless table before us. It's a buffet filled with an overflow of delicious morsels and unimaginable delights!

And the right to take part in this agapao, this marriage supper of God's affection, this type of love, it doesn't come from what we do, or how hard we work, or who we think we are. This love, this invitation to the spectacular marriage supper of the Lamb, comes from who He says we are and from what His Son has done for us!

When God promised that He would never leave us nor forsake us (Deuteronomy 31:6, Hebrews 13:5), He wasn't just making it up because it sounded eloquent. That is the actual love that He has for us!

We are never alone, never separated, even when the world tells us otherwise. Even when it feels otherwise, God is always there.

Wow.

That's remarkable. And it will flush away a lifetime of bad theology if you let it.

This is the type of love that took the first-century Church's breath away. It was a completely new way to understand God's passion for humanity, personified in Jesus Christ - the prophecy of His coming, His birth, His life, His death, His resurrection, and His sitting down at the right hand of the Father who adores his children.

It's a love that could not, would not stay in the grave, and would defy the physical rules of life with supernatural power and expectancy.

Jesus ... God ... loves you truly, madly, and deeply, and He will not stop loving you. Even if your world falls apart. Even if you are tortured or imprisoned unjustly, even if worldly circumstances begin to batter and bruise you, His Love for you will not, *cannot*, stop. His love is the foundation of everything for a true follower of Christ. This is a rock to build upon!

Because love is not an aspect of God.

God *is* love.

And love is so much more than what we have been taught. And God's love never changes (Hebrews 13:8).

And this is the love of a perfect Groom for His Bride.

Wedding bells

Seeing Jesus this way may be new to you.

I know it was for me.

Even though I had grown up in Christian households, and I had read the Bible back and forth plenty of times, I didn't understand Jesus this way. Even after leaving the faith and coming back to it years later, I still didn't know Him this way. I could argue, debate, revelate, preach, and pray with the best of them ... but I still didn't understand His love this way.

And in some ways, I didn't want to.

Intimacy is a terrifying word for those who have been deeply wounded. It was easier to clothe myself in rules and rituals, dogma, and judgment than opening up my heart for the grandest adventure I could ever imagine.

I knew the Scriptures. I knew what I had been told and taught. But I didn't have a true picture of His love. I had it locked in my head, but barely in my heart. All I could see was my sin, my shortcomings, how often I "missed the mark," how hard I was told I had to work, and how hard I was jockeying for a position in the "Christian world."

In truth, I looked at my relationship with Jesus as a worker-bee, always wondering what His will for my life was and jumping from task to task.

But that's not what Jesus wants. He wants so much more. He wanted me to rest in Him, with my head against His chest just as His favorite disciple did when He walked upon the Earth. Imagine it! What an intimate moment this was. Jesus' disciple was so close that he had his head resting upon Jesus' heart. This intimacy makes many of us so uncomfortable. This completely violates many modern notions of personal space and male-male interaction. But here it is, in Scripture, a disciple so enraptured with Jesus that his head lay upon Jesus' chest, and no one thinks otherwise. There is no scandal here. No embarrassment. This kind of intimacy with the King of kings was the norm.

And He wants that with you.

And He wants you to see yourself the way He sees you. And as far as His will for your life goes, His will is to be close to and know you. Jesus goes so far as to say that if we don't understand this, to know that it's all about knowing Him deeply, we are missing out on the kingdom He has for us! We can do everything in Jesus' name, but if it's not borne out of the intimate experience of Him, Jesus even says – *On that day many will say to me, 'Lord, Lord, did we not prophesy in your name, and cast out demons in your name, and do many mighty works in your name?' And then will I declare to them, "I never knew you"* (Matthew 7:22-23).

You can do all the amazing things in the world, but if you don't *know* Him intimately, it's all worthless and destined for destruction. You can learn about His love all day, but if you aren't realizing that love personally and releasing it to others, it's all for naught.

Imagine it this way. I can give you a book about the Church of the Holy Sepulcher in Jerusalem, often called the most beautiful church in the world. You can learn everything there is to know about it - height, dimensions, history, who worked on it, who designed it, all about the frescoes within it ... everything. Yet, for all that knowledge, if you don't go there yourself and experience it, you don't *know* it. You don't know how it smells. You don't know how the dust catches the light at a certain time of day when the sun streams through the windows. You don't know the interplay of the shadows and light on the paintings, deepening the atmosphere.

I can give you a book about love, and you can memorize everything there is to know about the book, learn the chemical reactions in the body, and the effect that love has on the mind. You can learn everything there is to know about love, even learn about the greatest lovers in history. But until you fully experience love for yourself, it's just knowledge in your head.

I can give you a book about God's love. You can memorize everything, chapter, and verse. But until you experience His love yourself, the love of a Groom for His bride, and the love of a bride for the Groom, your interpretation of His love will always be through someone else's eyes.

Until you know Jesus as the Groom, your view will always be askew.

The Invitation

There are many ways to view the Bible, and we all bring our personal biases into the reading of the text. But our world is suffering because we don't understand how to read the incredible words of the Bible through the lens of true Love - the unconditional love of a Husband for His bride.

There are many teachers and pastors who are amazing in their duties, but they don't know the love of the Groom. And this misunderstanding of God's love flows over to their unknowing congregations, muddying the waters of intimacy and connection.

Truth be told, many say they love Jesus but haven't experienced the fullness of His love.

But we can't fault them for that.

It's because they haven't been shown how. They haven't been led to true Love. They don't even know it's possible to be so free. They don't know what resting in Him looks like.

Jesus wants us to love Him with all of our heart, soul, mind, and strength, and love others as we love ourselves. And that means ALL the way, moving into union with Him as in a marriage. And that's because marriage is an earthly model of a heavenly reality—the reality of Christ's love for His Church.

Did you think it was a coincidence that Jesus' first public miracle occurred at a wedding? His transformation of 120 gallons of water into wine - the best wine available - symbolizes life recreated and raised to new levels, the best existence possible, a life given purpose and meaning where two realities become one.

Because there IS going to be a wedding.

And it's time for you to journey down the aisle.

So take a deep breath, and look deep into His eyes, where you can see the spiral of galaxies stretching into the infinity of His gaze.

He's already asked for your hand in marriage.

He's just waiting for you to accept the invitation.

Look at Him, standing at the end of the aisle, waiting in expectation. Jesus is looking at you with His wide smile. And there is longing in His gaze. For you. And if you look closely, you can see the tracks of tears. But they aren't tears of sadness. They are tears of joy. The bride is finally realizing who they are.

In the vast cathedral of the universe, the resounding chords of the Bridal Chorus reverberate a divine melody that has been composed since the beginning of time just for you. You are His. You've always been His. This is the most profound truth, the foundational essence of your being, your cherished reality.

In this sacred moment, the celestial realm is poised in reverence. Angels, radiant and resplendent, stand in awe, their golden-fire wings shimmering under the heavenly light. The Cloud of Witnesses, those souls who have walked their earthly journey before you, are standing too. Their eyes are bright with anticipation, their hearts pulsating in harmony with the celestial rhythm, as they eagerly await your procession down the divine aisle.

An aisle, not made of marble or stone, but of love and grace, stretches out before you. It is strewn with the petals of prayers whispered and blessings bestowed, leading you toward your eternal promise. Towards Him.

Your Groom is waiting, Jesus, the embodiment of pure, unconditional love. His hand, the one that shaped the cosmos, is outstretched, beckoning you to Him. His eyes, the mirrors of infinite compassion and eternal wisdom, sparkle with a love so profound, so encompassing, it eclipses all celestial bodies and makes even the wonder of creation seem pale in comparison.

It's time for you to step forth, to take your place by His side. A place that has been reserved for you since the genesis of existence, a place where you truly belong. As you take each step, remember, each footfall is a note in the symphony of love, a testament to your journey toward this pure union.

As you reach Him and your hand slips into His, a surge of holy love, stronger than any force in the universe, envelops you. At this moment, the heavens hold their breath. Time stands still, for the author of time holds your hand in His. And expectation whispers as love, in fullest form, is finally realized by His bride.

And thus begins the eternal dance, a dance of two becoming one, a dance that the universe has been waiting to witness since the thought of you flickered into flame in the Father's mind.

Today, you are not just a bride; you are His bride, united in divine love, forever and always.

Scripture References

Deuteronomy 31:6 - "Be strong and bold; have no fear or dread of them, because it is the Lord your God who goes with you; he will not fail you or forsake you."

Song of Songs 1:3 - "Your anointing oils are fragrant, your name is perfume poured out; therefore the maidens love you."

Isaiah 62:5 - "For as a young man marries a young woman, so shall your builder marry you, and as the bridegroom rejoices over the bride, so shall your God rejoice over you."

Matthew 22:37-39 - "He said to him, 'You shall love the Lord your God with all your heart, and with all your soul, and with all your mind.' This is the greatest and first commandment. And a second is like it: 'You shall love your neighbor as yourself.'"

John 3:16 - "For God so loved the world that he gave his only Son so that everyone who believes in him may not perish but may have eternal life."

John 3:19 - "And this is the judgment, that the light has come into the world, and people loved darkness rather than light because their deeds were evil."

John 13:34-35 - "I give you a new commandment, that you love one another. Just as I have loved you, you also should love one another. By this everyone will know that you are my disciples, if you have love for one another."

Romans 5:8 - "But God proves his love for us in that while we still were sinners Christ died for us."

Romans 8:38-39 - "For I am convinced that neither death, nor life, nor angels, nor rulers, nor things present, nor things to come, nor powers, nor height, nor depth, nor anything else in all creation, will be able to separate us from the love of God in Christ Jesus our Lord."

1 Corinthians 13:4-8 - "Love is patient; love is kind; love is not envious or boastful or arrogant or rude. It does not insist on its own way; it is not irritable or resentful; it does not rejoice in wrongdoing, but rejoices in the truth. It bears all things, believes all things, hopes all things, endures all things. Love never ends."

Galatians 3:28 - "There is no longer Jew or Greek, there is no longer slave or free, there is no longer male and female; for all of you are one in Christ Jesus."

Ephesians 1:4-5 - "just as he chose us in Christ before the foundation of the world to be holy and blameless before him in love. He destined us for adoption as his children through Jesus Christ, according to the good pleasure of his will."

Ephesians 3:17-19 - "and that Christ may dwell in your hearts through faith, as you are being rooted and grounded in love. I pray that you may have the power to comprehend, with all the saints, what is the breadth and length and height and depth, and to know the love of Christ that surpasses knowledge so that you may be filled with all the fullness of God."

Ephesians 5:25 - "Husbands, love your wives, just as Christ loved the church and gave himself up for her."

Colossians 3:14 - "Above all, clothe yourselves with love, which binds everything together in perfect harmony."

1 Peter 1:22 - "Now that you have purified your souls by your obedience to the truth so that you have genuine mutual love, love one another deeply from the heart."

1 John 4:7-12 - "Beloved, let us love one another, because love is from God; everyone who loves is born of God and knows God. Whoever does not love does not know God, for God is love. God's love was revealed among us in this way: God sent his only Son into the world so that we might live through him. In this is love, not that we loved God but that he loved us and sent his Son to be the atoning sacrifice for our sins. Beloved, since God loved us so much, we also ought to love one another. No one has ever seen God; if we love one another, God lives in us, and his love is perfected in us."

Revelation 19:7-9 - "Let us rejoice and exult and give him the glory, for the marriage of the Lamb has come, and his bride has made herself ready; to her it has been granted to be clothed with fine linen, bright and pure—for the fine linen is the righteous deeds of the saints. And the angel said to me, 'Write this: Blessed are those who are invited to the marriage supper of the Lamb.' And he said to me, 'These are true words of God.'"

Hebrews 13:5 - "Keep your lives free from the love of money, and be content with what you have; for he has said, 'I will never leave you or forsake you.'"

Hebrews 13:8 - "Jesus Christ is the same yesterday and today and forever."

Notes

Initial

_____

_____

_____

_____

_____

_____

_____

_____

_____

_____

_____

Later

_____

_____

_____

_____

_____

REVELATION FOUR

THE THIN PLACE

For thousands of years, humans have searched out sacred and mystical places for a taste of the divine. The pyramids, Stonehenge, Notre Dame, The Western Wall, and St Peter's Basilica – these are all places that light the fires of imagination, places where people feel they can reach out and potentially touch another world.

Almost every ancient culture holds a belief in Thin Places, places where the very fabric of physical reality intersected with that of the supernatural – places where a person can walk within two worlds, that of the sacred and secular, the transcendent and the common - places where two worlds become one.

Some describe Thin Places as spaces where humanity experiences God more often. Others are more fanciful with their language, describing Thin Places as locales where *the distance between heaven and Earth collapses.*

But for all their beauty, grandeur, and mystery, I have to smile to myself. For literal millennia, people have been coming to mystical places seeking to touch another world, searching for a touch of the divine.

But they are missing out.

For while there is a mystery to behold in these places, the truth is that stones and monuments can never be what you are.

Because you don't have to go anywhere to search out a Thin Place.

And right now, I will show you where the most powerful Thin Place you will ever personally experience is.

Are you ready?

Go find a mirror, look in it and say these mighty words – I AM the Thin Place.

Because you are the Thin Place where worlds collide!

The Bridge Between Worlds

One of the greatest lessons you will learn on your journey into intimacy is what you carry inside of you. When you begin to realize who you are and who your Father in Heaven is, and when you begin to know what His Son has done and made available to you, a monumental and tectonic shift begins to take place.

After all, when you embrace the fact that you have free and unfettered access to the ultimate power inside and outside the universe, and realize that power is inside of you? Things are going to start changing.

Because you are the Thin Place where the power of God, the love of the Father, and the resurrection power of the Holy Spirit come together.

YOU are the sacred place.

Yes, there are beautiful monuments people seek out for a touch of the divine. Yes, these places may be thousands of years old. Yes, places like the pyramids and Stonehenge may have the reputation of being touched by the gods. And yes, these ancient monuments may seem older than time itself.

But guess what is older?

You.

The real you. Not your flesh and bone body, but the spirit that dwells inside of you YOU

After all, God knew you before the foundation of the world, according to Ephesians 1:4.

And when we look at the Psalms and read 24:9 - *Lift up your heads, you gates; lift them up, you ancient doors, that the King of glory may come in –* guess what?

That's you.

The ultimate power of the universe dwells inside of you and through you. You are the gate that the King steps into this world through. The Creator, who created everything and created you in His image, has called you to realize who you are - an atmosphere changer, a releaser of His Glory and Presence so that His love and passion flow out of you like a river of Living Water because He is alive *in YOU.*

Your spirit is older than any ancient monument. And your spirit will still be around when those stones crumble to dust in a few million years. Your spirit, who you really are, exists outside of time in the Heavenly realm, raised up with and seated with Christ in Heavenly places in union with His Spirit (Ephesians 2:6).

And you are the Thin Place, where Heaven and Earth collide.

Fracturing the paradigm

I know this may be hard for you to accept, especially if you have been raised in a religious framework. After all, most of us are taught that we must seek something outside of ourselves to touch the divine. Or worse, we're taught that we are lowly worms who must work hard to become what God requires us to be. That we must act a certain way, talk a certain way, or jump through hoops to usher in the Kingdom of God. We are taught that sacred places are places we go or have to seek out, pay pilgrimage to, or have to build out of our own power.

But that's not what Jesus said.

After being asked when the Kingdom of God would come, in Luke 17:21, Jesus says, *The kingdom of God does not come with observation; nor will they say, 'See here!' or 'See there!' For indeed, the kingdom of God is within you.*

Now, let's take a pause.

If you're one of these people who likes to read as fast as possible, I encourage you to slow down here. Take a moment. Let's weigh the implications of what Jesus is saying.

The kingdom of God is within you.

Jesus isn't implying it. And He's not speaking in mystical terms. And this isn't a parable. Jesus is saying this as a statement of fact.

...the Kingdom of God is within you.

The spiritual realm over which God reigns as king of the universe exists not in some far-off land. It doesn't reside in a temple. And it is not a place you have to pay a pilgrimage to.

The Kingdom of God is within you.

But Jesus doesn't stop there.

In Matthew 6:33, Jesus says that the Kingdom of God is inside of you and *you must seek it.*

In Matthew 7:7-8, Jesus says the Kingdom is available to everyone who seeks it, it is within reach, and all you must do to access it is simply knock. There are no hoops to jump through. Nothing you have to sign, no program you have to join. All you have to do is have the desire to see the Kingdom and to take action.

And maybe most importantly, Ephesians 3:17, 2 Corinthians 13:5, Galatians 2:20, and Colossians 1:27 all refer to the Kingdom of God being in our midst and in the presence of Jesus, who is inside of each us!

The Kingdom of God won't be found by looking for it in a geographical location. It's not in monuments. And the sacred isn't locked in stones. Nor is the Kingdom of God about building giant cathedrals to house the Glory of God.

Rather, the kingdom exists in us. In our hearts. In our minds. In our souls and spirits.

And you are the space between worlds where these realities come together. Inside of you. Within you. You are the empowered lightning rod, the gate, the point of entry of the Kingdom of God into the reality of Earth.

And that's a big deal.

So, knowing the Kingdom of God is within, do you release that Kingdom into the earth and become a flowing river of Living Water ... or do you hold it all inside and become a stagnant Dead Sea?

The Moment of Release

There is a dramatic scene during Christ's crucifixion, where Jesus offers Himself up on the cross.

At the moment of Jesus' physical death, Jesus cries out loudly and yields His Spirit. And Matthew 27:51 tells us at that moment that *the curtain in the sanctuary of the Temple was torn in two, from top to bottom. The earth shook and rocks split apart.*

Most of us have heard this story. And sure, we read about it or see a dramatic re-enactment during Easter ceremonies and go, "Yeah! Power of God, baby!"

But this is the thing - there is so much in this moment for you in your journey of intimacy that you might be missing.

To the people of Jesus' day, the Temple of Jerusalem was all-important.

It was where people came to experience God, as this was where the Hebraic people believed that God held his Presence upon the earth. And it wasn't just Jews that came to the Temple. Gentiles were known to come and pay homage to the Israelite God as well. The Temple of Jerusalem was a sacred place, a Thin Place ... some would say THE Thin Place of ALL Thin Places.

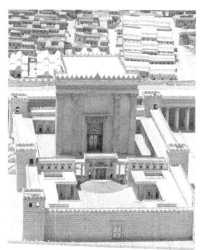

The Temple of Jerusalem

Herod the Great, recognized as the King of the Jews by the Roman Senate, had built the Temple of Jerusalem into a wonder of the ancient world. After being installed as king by the Roman government, Herod began a building campaign unrivaled in much of the ancient world, with the Temple of Jerusalem the focus of much of his attention. Building upon the modest temple that was rebuilt by the Jews returning from the Babylonian almost five centuries earlier, Herod transformed the temple structure into

an architectural marvel adorned with intricate edifices and ornate fa-
cades. Set upon a great fortified hill, the Temple was visible for miles,
shining as a polished white beacon of light, rising above Jerusalem.

But Herod didn't build the Temple of Jerusalem for God's glory. He built
it for his own glory and to improve his standing and place over the
people he ruled. Empowered by his support from Rome, Herod used
terror to subjugate those under his thumb. And Herod's reputation as a
murderous tyrant went far beyond the pages of the Bible. To maintain a
tight grip on his power, Herod even executed several of his children, and
his wife, Mariamne. His secret police were inserted across the political
and religious spectrum, even infiltrating the ruling classes of Israelite
priests. Scholars, leaders, and priests that spoke against him, even in
private, were slaughtered in public displays of power.

And while Herod had built the Temple of Jerusalem into a modern marvel, the grand building project had come at a great cost. The burden of
financing the glorious temple fell upon the people who needed it the
most. The populace was taxed heavily to pay for their temple. Money
was scarce, provision inadequate, and the people suffered for it.

Despite all this, the Temple of Jerusalem *was* a sacred place, and in
Jesus' day was the center of Hebraic life. All Jews were required to make
a pilgrimage to Jerusalem three times a year: in spring for Passover
(Pesach), in summer for the Feast of Weeks (Shavuot), and in the fall for
Tabernacles (Sukkot). And the Temple was the focal point of every Jew's
visit to Jerusalem.

The central part of the Temple was referred to as *The Holy of Holies*, the
earthly dwelling place of God's presence. And this interior part of the
temple was separated from the rest, a sacred space intended for God
alone. As it was believed that God could not be in the presence of sin,
no one was allowed to enter this space or it was believed the trespasser
would die instantly from God's holiness. Only the High Priest was allowed
in this space one day a year to make atonement for the sins of the people
on Yom Kippur. The floor, ceiling, and walls of this room were plated with

pure gold. And a giant veil separated this portion of the temple from its secondary portion.

The veil of separation was a blue, scarlet, and purple heavily embroidered curtain over four inches thick, sixty feet high, and thirty feet wide. And embroidered on the veil were *"all the things that were mystical in the heavens,"* according to Josephus in his <u>Antiquities of the Jews</u>.

Outside of the massive veil, the rest of the interior temple proper was set up similarly to Moses' tabernacle in the wilderness - a golden altar of incense, a golden table of showbread, and

the golden lampstand. Considered sacred, but not necessarily filled with God's Glory like the Holy of Holies, only the daily priest on duty was allowed to enter this area.

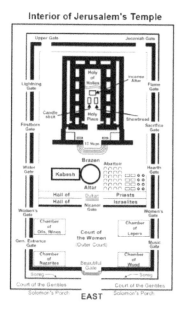

Interior of Jerusalem's Temple

Outside the core temple was the Inner Court, comprised of the Court of Priests, the Court of Israel, and the Court of Women. The inner portion of the Inner Court was the Court of Priests, where only priests were allowed and where they offered sacrifice.

The next area was for ceremonially clean Jewish men, called the Court of Israel.

The area outside of that, through the Nicanor gate, was the Court of the Women. Women were not allowed to go past this point; this court was where women and not ritually pure men could make voluntary offerings.

And outside the Inner Court was the Outer Court, also called the Court of Gentiles. This is where non-Jewish people could come to worship or pay homage to the Israelite God. But Gentiles were not allowed to go past this point. And if a Gentile attempted to enter the inner court from the outer court, the penalty was death.

To the Jewish people, the Temple was very serious business.

In our 21st-century mindset, it is difficult to imagine the importance of the Temple to the Jewish people. The Temple was the literal center of Hebrew spiritual and religious life. It symbolized their deep connection with God and, to them, was the holiest location on Earth. The Temple of Jerusalem is where the Hebrews, the descendants of Abraham, the first person to make a covenant with God, came together to worship and offer sacrifices to the one true God.

The Temple not only represented the Jews' devotion to God but also served as a physical reminder of their unique and enduring identity that dated back a thousand years. The Temple of Jerusalem was a beacon of hope for the Jewish people, symbolizing their resilience and strength in the face of adversity. The Temple was their link to God and revealed to the world that they were Yahweh's chosen people.

The Veil of Separation

But I want to take you back into the Holy of Holies, journeying through the hallowed courts, halls, and corridors, and back to the massive curtain that set apart the space where God's Presence held a place on Earth.

Within the sacred halls of the Temple of Jerusalem, the veil of separation served as the ethereal boundary guarding the sanctity of the Holy of Holies, the temple's innermost and most sacred sanctum. Upon entering the chamber, you would immediately face a secondary curtain hanging 18 inches from the inner curtain. This was to protect the massive inner curtain from the view of those who have not been made ritually pure. The outer curtain embraced the south side, while the inner curtain adorned the north, forming a mystical corridor reserved solely for the high priest on his sacred journey into the Holy of Holies on Yom Kippur.

Josephus, the first-century Jewish historian, chronicled Herod's ambitious expansion of the temple, raising its celestial height to an awe-inspiring 40 cubits (or 60 feet). Jewish tradition speaks of the veil's immense weight, which demanded the strength of 300 priests to carefully lift and hang it, emphasizing the impenetrable separation between the Holy of Holies and the mortal world.

This curtain wasn't some flimsy, wispy, translucent billowing curtain. This was a 4-inch-thick, 60-foot-high fabric wall that took 300 men to move! If it happened to fall, it would kill those underneath. And it was this veil that was violently torn by God's Presence breaking forth, the whole thing torn asunder top down by God's power! The very curtain that separated God's Holy Presence from the ritually impure was rent apart, and no longer would there be separation, literal or symbolic, from God and His children! The literal fabric that symbolized sacredness and space-time, all things mystical in the Heavens, was ripped apart by God upon Jesus yielding up His Spirit in Matthew 27:51!

God's presence wasn't just going to reside in a temple, hidden behind a double curtain, and only visited one day out of the year by a high priest. Now, God's children were going to have the potential to carry the Father's very Presence, every...single...day

The Thin Place Where Worlds Collide

There is a mystery of intimacy waiting to be revealed when we look at the design of the Temple of Jerusalem.

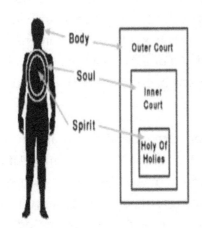

Just as the Temple of Jerusalem was made of three basic parts – the outer court, the inner court, and the Holy of Holies, in 1 Thessalonians 5:23, Paul says that we are made of three basic components – a body, a soul, and a spirit. So comparatively, your body is symbolic to the outer court, your soul the inner court, and the spirit the Holy of Holies.

As you begin this journey of intimacy, part of understanding your absolute closeness with the divine creator of the universe is realizing the truth of where you are right now.

Because you might think that you are only here on Earth right now. You might think that you exist only in the space you are taking up physically. But the New Testament teaches differently:

> *but God, who is rich in mercy, out of the great love with which*
> *he loved us even when we were dead through our trespasses,*
> *made us alive together with Christ—by grace you have been*
> *saved— and raised us up with him and seated us with him in*
> *the heavenly places in Christ Jesus, so that in the ages to come*
> *he might show the immeasurable riches of his grace in kindness*
> *toward us in Christ Jesus. - Ephesians 2:4-7*

You're not just on Earth. Your spirit is *right now seated in Christ in Heavenly places.* And if your spirit is indeed seated in Christ and Jesus is within you, guess what? The veil of separation between your spirit and that of Christ is indeed torn!

You are now God's home on Earth.

You are now God's temple.

You have the holy of Holies within you where His presence resides!

But if all this sounds crazy, don't just take my word for it -

- *Do you not know that you are a temple of God and that the Spirit of God dwells in you?* (1 Corinthians 3:16)

- *Or do you not know that your body is the temple of the Holy Spirit within you, whom you have from God? You are not your own, for you were bought with a price. So glorify God in your body* (1 Cor 6:19-20)

- *In whom the whole structure, being joined together, grows into a holy temple in the Lord. In him you also are being built together into a dwelling place for God by the Spirit* (Ephesians 2:21-22)

- *And you are living stones that God is building into His spiritual temple. What's more, you are His holy priests* (1 Peter 2:5)

And don't forget what Jesus Himself said – *The Kingdom of God is within YOU* (Luke 17:20-21)

You are the thin place.

You are united with Jesus, and He lives in you. He is in union with you.

You are God's holy temple. You are the Ark of the Covenant. You are the Mercy Seat of Christ in this world.

All of these things that were outside in the Old Covenantal system are now INSIDE you. The veil has been torn. The Holy Spirit moves through your Spirit, which is seated in Christ, through your soul, and to your physical body to be released, literally changing the world with your Presence because of the work done through Christ Jesus!

When you know whose you are and who you are, you don't have to go to Thin Places. You just have to look in a mirror!

You are the Thin Place where the heartbeat and rhythm of your Creator thrums.

The Torn Veil

You don't have to travel to rocks on top of hills, and you don't have to go climb pyramids; you don't have to sit in a circle and chant kumbaya, rub crystals together, or go on pilgrimages to holy places. And you don't have to go to the hot new conference or the prophet of the month to experience God.

And when you feel like God is far away, all you have to do is gently remind yourself that that's your imagination telling you a lie. Because there is no separation. The veil has been torn apart, and God never stitched it back together. You are the Thin Place where Heaven intersects with Earth.

Now, does that mean that other earthly Thin Places aren't real? By no means. Yes, places do have power. Certain places "do" carry a certain atmosphere. But God doesn't house Himself in places on Earth:

> He is the God who made the world and everything in it. Since he is Lord of heaven and earth, he doesn't live in man-made temples, and human hands can't serve his needs—for he has no needs. He himself gives life and breath to everything, and he satisfies every need   -Acts 17:24-25

I'm not saying there are no earthly Thin Places. But I AM saying that you'll never experience a Thin Place greater than the one you yourself are. For God houses Himself in you.

And did you notice what else happened in Matthew 27:51? Not only was the veil of the Holy of Holies torn in two from top to bottom, but the earth shook and the rocks split. And this is important. The very things that the ancients believed held the power of God, things that people made idols from such as wood and stone, were shaken and ripped apart as well.

Because God doesn't live in stones and pieces of wood. Yes, they are a part of creation. But God isn't in them.

God is in you.

Where Heaven Enters Earth

You are the Thin Place. You are the place where Heaven and Earth collide.

And sure, this is all good stuff. But it's fair to ask, how do you experience this for yourself? Especially when you have been told all of your life that God is far away and that you have to work yourself into his favor.

The first step for this part of your journey is to acknowledge that it's true - you are a Thin Place.

Find that mirror again and take a look.

Follow the lines of your face, your eyes, your cheeks, your jaw, your mouth, and your nose. Realize that you are fearfully and wonderfully made and created to be a dwelling place of God's love.

Now say that out loud - fearfully and wonderfully made and created to be a dwelling place of God's love.

Don't worry. All of that shame and your discounting of yourself, that's all a lie. Let it go.

Keep saying it.

Tell yourself that you are the Thin Place until you begin to receive it. You have the chance to step through the door that the Lord has placed before you. *Lift up your heads, you gates; lift them up, you ancient doors, that the King of glory may come in.*

Step through. Listen and see how much God loves you.

Say it until you feel that love beginning to bubble underneath your skin, making you smile. Or cry. Letting that cool rush or fiery warmth flush out every lie you've ever told yourself about that person in the mirror.

And say it until you believe it - You are loved. You are His.

You are the Thin Place where Heaven and Earth collide, releasing Living Waters into the world.

Scripture References

Psalms 24:7 - "Lift up your heads, you gates; lift them up, you ancient doors, that the King of glory may come in."

Psalms 24:9 - "Lift up your heads, you gates; lift them up, you ancient doors, that the King of glory may come in."

Psalm 139:14 - "I praise you because I am fearfully and wonderfully made; your works are wonderful, I know that full well."

Matthew 6:33 - "Seek first the kingdom of God."

Matthew 7:7-8 - "Ask, and it will be given to you; seek, and you will find; knock, and the door will be opened to you."

Matthew 27:51 - "The curtain in the sanctuary of the Temple was torn in two, from top to bottom."

Luke 17:20-21 - "The kingdom of God is within you."

John 14:20 - "On that day you will know that I am in my Father, and you in me, and I in you."

Acts 17:24-25 - "The God who made the world and everything in it... doesn't live in man-made temples..."

Romans 8:9-11 - "But you are not in the flesh; you are in the Spirit, since the Spirit of God dwells in you."

1 Corinthians 3:16-17 - "Do you not know that you are God's temple and that God's Spirit dwells in you? If anyone destroys God's temple, God will destroy that person."

1 Corinthians 6:17 - "But anyone united to the Lord becomes one spirit with him."

1 Corinthians 6:19-20 - "Do you not know that your bodies are temples of the Holy Spirit, who is in you, whom you have received from God?"

2 Corinthians 6:16 - "For we are the temple of the living God; as God said, 'I will live in them and walk among them, and I will be their God, and they shall be my people.'"

2 Corinthians 13:5 - "Examine yourselves to see whether you are living in the faith."

Galatians 2:20 - "I have been crucified with Christ; it is no longer I who live, but Christ who lives in me."

Ephesians 1:4 - "God knew you before the foundation of the world."

Ephesians 2:4-7 - "God, who is rich in mercy, made us alive together with Christ and raised us up with him and seated us with him in the heavenly places."

Ephesians 2:6 - "Raised up with and seated with Christ in Heavenly places."

Ephesians 2:10 - "For we are God's handiwork, created in Christ Jesus to do good works, which God prepared in advance for us to do."

Ephesians 2:21-22 - "In him you also are being built together into a dwelling place for God by the Spirit."

Ephesians 3:17 - "Christ may dwell in your hearts."

Colossians 1:27 - "Christ in you, the hope of glory."

1 Thessalonians 5:23 - "May your whole spirit, soul, and body be kept blameless at the coming of our Lord Jesus Christ."

Hebrews 10:19-20 - "Therefore, my friends, since we have confidence to enter the sanctuary by the blood of Jesus, by the new and living way that he opened for us through the curtain (that is, through his flesh)."

1 Peter 2:5 - "You yourselves like living stones are being built up as a spiritual house."

Notes

Initial
_____

_____

_____

_____

_____

_____

_____

_____

_____

_____

_____

_____

Later
_____

_____

_____

_____

_____

REVELATION FIVE

THE SECRET PLACE

I n the Scriptures, ancient prophets and mystics of old speak of a mystical refuge called the Secret Place. But this enigmatic sanctuary is not anchored to any geographical location, nor can it be found on a map. The Secret Place exists in the deepest recesses of the human soul, waiting to be discovered by those who yearn for a connection with God.

In the lofty language of the Psalms, The Secret Place is an enticing oasis, where the weary traveler lays down their burdens to be rejuvenated by the embrace of the Most High. Here, the hustle and bustle of the outside world dissolve into a distant murmur, replaced by the soothing whispers of eternity.

The Secret Place is a sanctuary, where the veil of separation separating the temporal and the divine is non-existent, allowing for a profound communion with the Creator. The Secret Place is where the heart and soul find solace, a haven where the deepest questions, fears, and aspirations can be laid bare before the Almighty.

In the Secret Place, the divine tapestry of the cosmos is revealed, as the wisdom of the ages is unfurled before the seeker's eyes. This ethereal realm is a treasure trove of spiritual discovery, where the transcendent power of faith is brought to life, igniting a passion for God that burns brightly within the soul.

And the Secret Place is an invitation to embark on a transformative journey, to explore the uncharted depths of the human spirit and unearth the priceless riches that lie within. And the deeper you dive into this captivating realm, the more you explore, the more you will be forever changed.

It is a Secret Place made possible by a bridegroom – where you can dwell to commune and partner with your Creator. A place of protection and safety, but more than that, *a place of intimacy and adoration.*

But few enter the Secret Place knowingly. Even fewer know such a place exists, their Secret Place buried under distractions, and hidden under misconceptions. Its entrances are concealed by a lack of intimate teaching.

But after this session, we will open the door of your own Secret Place, a Bridal Chamber, prepared for you to delight in and enter into *incredible union with God Himself.*

The Secret Place Revealed

In various translations of the Bible, the Secret Place is mentioned over 15 times.

Psalms 27 and 31 mention the Secret Place as a very real place of protection, where God offers His shelter to a believer in need. As God's children,

Scripture says that we are offered a place of warmth and security in the Father's arms, where we are always welcome and protected against what can often be a cold and unsafe world.

Psalm 91 goes even further, opening with the epic line, *"He who dwells in the secret place of the Most High shall abide under the shadow of the Almighty."* This Scripture is found in homes, and churches, and is written on the covers of more journals than we could ever count. It's a beautiful promise of protection, God's favor, and love for us, even in times of suffering and pain. Just as a young child runs to their parent in times of need, we can run to the arms of our Father any time we choose to.

And because the Secret Place is written of as so enticing, this mysterious place has become something people strive for. Endless books are available to teach you how to find it. Sermons have been spoken of how to attain it. Some say you have to have a physical prayer closet to enter it. Others teach you have to endure endless works to gain access to it. And even worse, some people think that because of their poor choices, they aren't even allowed in, and believe they have to fast or serve penance to enter.

But what if entry into the Secret Place isn't a great mystery and has been right inside, lying undetected before you, just waiting for you to find the key to enter whenever you desire? What if accessing it wasn't difficult? And most importantly, *what if the Secret Place is more than just a place of safety*, and its purpose is deeper than we've been told or ever dreamed?

When beginning your journey of intimacy with your Creator, there's an essential lesson you must come to understand. Your journey will never be complete until you learn to dwell with God in the Secret Place.

And step one is to realize that the Secret Place between you and God is very real.

When Moses asked to see God's Glory in Exodus 33, God told Moses that no man could see Him and live. So, God allowed Moses to see his Glory in passing from the Secret Place, put Moses in a cleft in the rock, and covered him with his hand until he passed.

It sounds daunting, doesn't it? No man can see God and live? How in the world can we be intimate with such a Being?

But pause. Take a breath. Recall that because of Jesus, the veil has been torn. We now exist in a New Covenant, where we are made righteous in Christ (2 Corinthians 5:21; Romans 3:22).

We are now boldly invited into his Presence with our heads held high.

And when *we* want to experience God's Presence, the Secret Place of the heart *is where we go* to experience His Glory.

But we're not just invited to go into the Secret Place occasionally. The promise that God offers us is the opportunity to *dwell* there. It is a place of meeting that He has prepared for us. It's a place where, no matter what is happening in the outside world, within our Secret Place with God, we can always be open, honest, and trust in Him.

In Matthew 6:6, Jesus said, *"When you pray, go into your room, close the door, and pray to your Father, who is unseen."* And news flash here. Jesus was not talking about a physical location. How do we know? Jesus spent plenty of time in the Secret Place communing with His Father. But Jesus also said, *"The Son of Man has no place to lay His head."* And if He didn't have somewhere to lay his head, chances are He didn't have a prayer closet set up.

When Jesus spoke of going to your room, He was speaking of the Secret Place.

In Acts 16, the Secret Place is what the apostles entered into when they sang songs of praise in prison, which later enabled miracles to break forth.

And the Secret Place was where Paul entered, where he was taught by the Lord Himself for 3 years after his conversion (Galatians 1:12).

This same Secret Place place is open to ALL believers. And the truth is, you don't need to do a single thing to access it other than to seek Him and REST in Him.

Jesus did not say, *If you come to me hungry you must fast for forty days before I feed you*, or *If you are thirsty, you must spend the day on your knees before I give you a drink*. He didn't say, *You must sit in silence for three days before you can hear My voice*. And Jesus NEVER said, *If you knock, I will only answer on Sunday*.

Jesus never gave *any* condition for entering *His Presence*.

Jesus said:

- those who come to Him will be fed (John 6:35; Psalm 22:26),

- those who are thirsty will be satisfied (Matthew 5:6; Psalm 107:9)

- those who listen for Him will hear (Matthew 11:15; John 10:27-28)

And most importantly, if we knocked, then the door would be open to us (Matthew 7:7). That's not to mention dozens of other verses in the Bible by prophets, disciples, and apostles who promised the same thing - including if we sought Him that we would find Him and be rewarded (Hebrews 11:6).

Here are the beautiful facts. Not one of Jesus' promises is contingent on you undergoing any rituals, going to sacred sites, making pilgrimages, performing works, suffering, or striving. And there are no ... ZERO ... conditions upon entering the Secret Place with Him.

When your children hurt themselves, do you require them to jump through any hoops to run into your arms?

When your partner needs you, do you require them to perform rituals or undergo dietary restrictions to find you?

What makes us think that God, who loves us more infinitely than WE could EVER love anything or anyone else, would make us do those things to enter into His place of meeting?

Remember the Thin Place? God physically tore the curtain of supposed separation in two, top to bottom. And I promise you, there is no indication in Scripture or otherwise that He re-stitched it together and hung it back up!

And because of that, we can enter the Secret Place of INTIMACY anytime we desire.

The Song of Intimacy

Intimacy.

It's a scary word and a huge deal. And intimacy with God is something most of us lack. And this is the crux of why most Christians miss out on the beauty of the Secret Place.

Because we lack intimacy with God, and because we don't know how to access the Secret Place of the Most High, we use religion, rituals, and rules to try and attain our desires instead.

But the beauty of the Gospel is its simplicity.

And instead of jumping through hoops to enter the Secret Place with God, you must realize that Jesus Himself is the key – He is the way, the truth, and the life.

Doctrine and dogmas aren't THE truth. Our rules and regulations aren't THE truth. Our leaders aren't THE truth. People on video screens aren't THE truth. And book authors aren't THE truth.

JESUS IS THE TRUTH.

The Secret Place is where we can meet Him and experience Him intimately is so much more than what we've ever dreamed ... because safety and security are only part of what happens when we enter.

And to prove this, I want to show you something.

Do you have a Bible nearby? I want you to pick it up and open it to the center. Chances are you will come across a book that's not brought up very often in church services and is rarely brought up in study groups.

Many teachers are uncomfortable discussing it.

Most pastors ignore it completely.

But it is a book essential to revealing the truth about your journey. Because this book is a love song that God has written for *you*.

And this book is called The Song of Solomon.

The Song of Solomon weaves an enigmatic melody, echoing the profound depths of two beings entwined in a sacred union, their hearts pulsating with an all-consuming love for one another.

This mesmerizing ode to love, both pure and holy, transcends the confines of ancient perceptions of intimacy. But even greater, The Song of Solomon unveils the divine love that Jesus seeks to share with you. The metaphors of marriage and romantic love embody the profound connection Jesus yearns to establish with you in this very moment.

Now in case you missed that, I'm going to repeat it.

The Song of Solomon is the song of the connection that Jesus yearns for with YOU.

Yes. The God of the Universe. The Word upon the Father's lips before the foundation of the world, the one who wove intricate and awe-inspiring patterns into the fabric of the cosmos. The One who sculpted the heavens and earth, giving birth to symphonies of celestial wonders across every realm and reality. The Creator of the elements, the laws of physics, quantum realities, and the frequencies and murmurs of the deep. The Triune God.

It is He that yearns for an intimate connection with you.

Right now.

The Song of Solomon reveals a shepherd king, whose heart becomes enraptured by a humble commoner – a woman who perceives herself unworthy of the king's adoring gaze, ill at ease within her own skin. She implores him not to look upon her, lamenting her darkness.

Yet, the king's vision pierces through her perceived inadequacies. Time and time again, He reassures her of her innate beauty and loveliness, gently shattering the walls of her disbelief. He doesn't hold her self-perceived thoughts against her. Instead, He tells her who she truly is to Him.

Sound familiar?

How many times has God's love and desire for you been mentioned just in this little book? And how many times when reading of this love have you skipped right past it? Or worse, had the thought that you don't deserve His love because of what you have done?

Let's face it. Sometimes, it's hard to believe we are loved by God. Sure, we hear it in our head, and yes, it sounds great, but we don't know it in our hearts. Like the shepherd king in the Song of Solomon, it is Jesus who reveals His love for us and breaks down our walls. Because He loved us first (1 John 4:19).

Yet if you don't come to know Jesus intimately, your experience of His love will never move past head knowledge to heart experience.

This is why the Song of Solomon is so important to knowing Him, and why abiding in His Presence in the Secret Place is essential. We may feel unworthy, but the love of Jesus cleanses us of the lies we believe. In the Secret Place, we come face to face with the fact that in Jesus' eyes, we are beautiful.

In the Secret Place, the Bridal Chamber, we realize our love is invincible and eternal. This is where we *realize I am my beloved's and my beloved is mine* (Song of Solomon 5:10 – 8:14). And it is in the Secret Place that this love is made manifest.

But here is the thing.

The sad truth is that most of us are just plain ole' uncomfortable with the intimacy of Song of Songs.

And this is because our current cultural views of sex and marriage have chucked the marriage bed under layers of shame and neglect. Discussing intimacy in marriage is often considered taboo in church services or study group settings. Because of the proliferation of pornography and sexuality in our culture, what was meant to be an incredible experience of two becoming one is rarely discussed, and the idea of intimacy with God has been tossed by the wayside.

Yet, the Song of Songs is about the union of Christ and His bride in the Secret Place, His pursuit of us into the Bridal Chamber, and the intimacy He desires with us. There's nothing pornographic about that. It's beautiful! After all, God says the marriage bed is pure (Hebrews 13:4). Even the great 1st-century Hebrew scholar Rabbi Akiva said, *"The greatest day was the one on which Israel received the Song of Songs. All of the writings in the Bible are holy and the Song of Songs is the holiest of holies."*

Because of our hyper-sexualization as a culture, instead of seeing the double meaning of the ancient love poetry of the Song of Songs, we jump to imagining physical copulation between Jesus and His Bride. But that is indeed silly. What Jesus promises us in the Secret Place makes physical sex as bland as possible. In the Secret Place, we are offered the chance to participate in a feast of spiritual pleasure so deep that it is life-altering.

Let's face it; it's easy for us to see our relationship with Christ as Him being our shepherd, our master, our friend, our savior, and our Lord. But the deepest relationship we are called to with Christ is with Him as the Bridegroom, hence the dozens and dozens of Scriptures referencing this point!

And what exactly is it that brides and bridegrooms do in their Bridal Chamber, their Secret Place?

Two become one.

And this is the true value of the Secret Place.

The Yearning of the Secret Place

Knowing the love of Jesus this way, as the desiring of union the Lord has for us in the Secret Place, will redefine your journey in every way. When we realize there is a place where we can experience the Creator of the universe drawing near, we begin to see ourselves how God sees us. And the fruit of the Spirit – love, joy, peace, patience, kindness, goodness, faithfulness, gentleness, and self-control begins to bloom, and our true self, our truest identity, begins to take root!

And most importantly, when we intimately know the undefeatable and eternal passion the King has for us, we begin to glimpse our lives from His eternal perspective.

We begin to see that God falls in love with us daily, and we have infinite reasons to fall in love with Him, no matter our circumstances or pain. We begin to see the blessings all around us, and never to overlook the beauty He gives us.

It's a realization that the God of the Universe, the creator of the elements, the one who put the stars into a spiral motion to mimic the dance steps

He made with the Son and the Holy Spirit at the dawn of time, the God who dances over us … He can choose to be anywhere He pleases.

And he chooses to DWELL with YOU in the Secret Place in your heart.

He chose you. And He chose me.

Any way you slice it, that's an amazing God.

And like the shepherd king of Song of Songs, He never promised a life without pain. And he never promised a lack of tragedy. He didn't promise laughter without sorrow, nor the light of the sun with no rain.

But Romans 8 does say that He will *never leave you nor forsake you; and that neither death, nor life, nor angels, nor principalities, nor powers, nor things present, nor things to come, nor height, nor depth, nor any other creature, shall be able to separate us from the love of God, which is in Christ Jesus our Lord.*

Close your eyes and breathe. Feel the air enter your nose, pulling down into your lungs. As your chest expands with the breath of God, feel the warmth move from within your belly to your fingers and toes. Every breath takes you deeper, and you are aware that as you breathe, your focus on the world begins to fall away. The concerns of your past drift off. The worries about your future seem less immediate. With every breath, you become more aware of the now.

And this is where Jesus wants to see you.

Now listen. Listen beyond your breathing. Listen inside.

For in the depths within, a realm of mystery calls, inviting you to venture forth.

The Secret Place whispers.

Seek, and you shall uncover its secrets. Ask, and the door shall swing wide for you. The Bridal Chamber, the sanctum of divine union, lies within your reach.

Step closer and dare to knock.

Close your eyes, and with a gentle touch, feel the door yield to your desire. Once within, marvel at the wonders that come alive.

Behold the magnificence of your Sacred Chamber, adorned by God for you alone. A sanctuary where your soul and the Creator unites, enraptured by unimaginable delights. A celestial banquet awaits, with the cosmos as your playground. Spiral galaxies illuminate your haven, while the earth serves as a mere footstool.

And there, amidst the splendor, He stands with open arms beckoning for you to rest your weary head within His tender embrace.

Share your fears and worries, and let His soothing whispers reveal your true essence.

In this sacred space, time holds no sway. Here, the finite and the eternal converge, and moments stretch into eternity while hours vanish like a fleeting breath.

Embrace the wonder of your new beginning and let the mysteries of the Secret Place entwine your heart and soul.

And what happens here is for you and Jesus alone.

Scripture References

Song of Solomon – All of it. Just read all of it. Swim in its beauty.

Exodus 33:18-23 - "Moses said, 'Show me your glory, I pray.' And he said, 'I will make all my goodness pass before you, and will proclaim before you the name, "The Lord"; and I will be gracious to whom I will be gracious, and will show mercy on whom I will show mercy. But,' he said, 'you cannot see my face; for no one shall see me and live.' And the Lord continued, 'See, there is a place by me where you shall stand on the rock; and while my glory passes by I will put you in a cleft of the rock, and I will cover you with my hand until I have passed by; then I will take away my hand, and you shall see my back; but my face shall not be seen.'"

Psalm 91:1 - "You who live in the shelter of the Most High, who abide in the shadow of the Almighty."

Matthew 6:6 - "But whenever you pray, go into your room and shut the door and pray to your Father who is in secret; and your Father who sees in secret will reward you."

Acts 16:25-26 - "About midnight Paul and Silas were praying and singing hymns to God, and the prisoners were listening to them. Suddenly there was an earthquake, so violent that the foundations of the prison were shaken; and immediately all the doors were opened and everyone's chains were unfastened."

Galatians 1:12 - "For I did not receive it from a human source, nor was I taught it, but I received it through a revelation of Jesus Christ."

Matthew 7:7 - "Ask, and it will be given you; search, and you will find; knock, and the door will be opened for you."

John 6:35 - "Jesus said to them, 'I am the bread of life. Whoever comes to me will never be hungry, and whoever believes in me will never be thirsty.'"

Matthew 5:6 - "Blessed are those who hunger and thirst for righteousness, for they will be filled."

Matthew 11:15 - "Let anyone with ears listen!"

Hebrews 11:6 - "And without faith, it is impossible to please God, for whoever would approach him must believe that he exists and that he rewards those who seek him."

John 10:27-28 - "My sheep hear my voice. I know them, and they follow me. I give them eternal life, and they will never perish. No one will snatch them out of my hand."

Psalm 22:26 - "The poor shall eat and be satisfied; those who seek him shall praise the Lord. May your hearts live forever!"

Matthew 11:28 - "Come to me, all you that are weary and are carrying heavy burdens, and I will give you rest."

2 Corinthians 5:21 - "For our sake he made him to be sin who knew no sin, so that in him we might become the righteousness of God."

Romans 3:22 - "For there is no distinction, since all have sinned and fall short of the glory of God; they are now justified by his grace as a gift, through the redemption that is in Christ Jesus."

Romans 8:38-39 - "For I am convinced that neither death, nor life, nor angels, nor rulers, nor things present, nor things to come, nor powers, nor height, nor depth, nor anything else in all creation, will be able to separate us from the love of God in Christ Jesus our Lord."

Notes

Initial
_____
_____
_____
_____
_____
_____
_____
_____
_____
_____
_____
_____

Later
_____
_____
_____
_____
_____

REVELATION SIX

THE HIDDEN TREASURE

G old coins. Jewels. And hidden treasures.

People spend their lives searching for them. And some have sacrificed everything trying to gain it.

Stories of hidden treasure have long captivated the human imagination, creating a mysterious allure that transcends time and cultures. The very notion of undiscovered riches, be it ancient artifacts, lost doubloons, or sunken treasures, taps into our innate sense of adventure and curiosity. They evoke a sense of possibility, igniting dreams of stumbling upon untold wealth or unlocking ancient secrets. And the allure of hidden treasure extends beyond material gain. It represents a quest for discovery, a desire to unravel the mysteries of the past and the thrill of the hunt.

The tales of famous missing treasures, such as the Ark of the Covenant, Aztec gold, or the Oak Island mystery, continue to capture our imagination. These legends are woven into the very fabric of human history, blending fact and fiction, inspiring countless adventurers, explorers, and treasure hunters to embark on quests in search of these elusive treasures.

For as long as humanity has existed, hidden treasures have been a hot topic, enticing imaginations and fueling dreams. The greatest expeditions ever sent out have been searching for precious metals and stones, and civilizations have risen and fallen on finding treasures ... and losing them.

But what if I told you that the greatest treasures are not hidden in caves, under the sands, or beneath the seas? What if gold coins and precious stones were everywhere around you, just waiting to be revealed - changing not just your life, but those of *everyone* you know? But not just that, what if you found that because of your growing intimacy with Christ, you have the map that unlocks the greatest hidden treasures the world has ever known?

The Greatest Treasure

Jesus loved tales of finding treasure. Ever the master storyteller, Jesus used parables of seeking treasure to explain what the Kingdom of God and the Father's love were like, where the characters involved took an active role in searching out items of worth - items that were lost but then found, and often purchased with great price.

As you have just begun your journey into intimacy with your Creator, I'm sure you've already come to realize that intimately knowing Jesus is a treasure in itself.

The journey of intimacy is an invitation to know the heart of the King of the Universe. You are invited into union, where our God says *I delight in you as a bridegroom rejoices over His bride,* and in reply, you have the honor to say *I am my beloved and my beloved is mine.*

It's amazing what falling in love does, doesn't it? It's a complete reality shift.

But here is something else - When you're in love and read His Scriptures, your eyes and ears will often reveal Jesus' words differently than you may have been taught. And this is because intimacy gives a deeper meaning to Jesus' sayings:

> *But blessed are your eyes, because they see; and your ears, because they hear. I tell you the truth, many prophets and righteous people longed to see what you see, but they didn't see it. And they longed to hear what you hear, but they didn't hear it* -Matthew 13:16-17

When you know Him deeply, everything changes.

And even stories of gold and treasure take on a richer meaning.

The Key

When Jesus used parables to speak of treasure and of searching for hidden things, they were often mentioned as metaphors for His Kingdom.

> *The kingdom of heaven is like a treasure hidden in the field, which a man found and hid again; and from joy over it he goes and sells all that he has and buys that field. Again, the kingdom of heaven is like a merchant seeking fine pearls, and upon finding one pearl of great value, he went and sold all that he had and bought it* – Matt 13:44-45

Most people are taught parables like this one are about discovering God's Kingdom and giving up everything one has to possess it. And this isn't wrong. This is correct! When we search for His Kingdom and find it, we want nothing more!

But here is the thing.

Most teachings STOP there.

Why?

Because we aren't seeing and listening with the wide-open eyes and ears of love, and we don't understand who we are in His sight. But when we understand that the veil is truly rent and that we are continually united with Christ on His throne, and within the Secret Place, we can unlock the mysteries of His greatest treasure.

But let's go a little deeper and get to the root of something nasty most of us believe. Most of us in the Christian world have a greater fear of judgment than we do an understanding of love. We're taught that our sins build a wall between us and Christ and that through our striving, we can hopefully enter His kingdom *when we die.*

Maybe. If we're lucky and catch God on a day He is in a good mood.

But here's the worse part. Because we are taught to think that God feels that way about us, it follows that He must think that way about everyone else, too.

But does that sound like Good News to you?

That doesn't sound like the Gospel that set the early Church's world on fire, does it?

The truth is - *For God so loved the world that HE gave his only begotten Son.* And I've said it before and will say it again - Jesus didn't walk the world in the flesh to change God's mind about us. God loves His creation. Jesus came to change the world's mind about God and reveal His Glory and Love through the Son.

And when we discover our treasured value in God's sight, all of a sudden, like Paul and Silas, we can sit in prison in chains, yet still enjoy the Lord's Presence, knowing who we are in His heart.

Jesus didn't die and rise again for trash. Jesus didn't come to release healing, hope, and love to create simple clay vases and worker bees.

Jesus came and is coming for *His Bride*, who He loves and adores. And that, my friend, is some real TREASURE!

And in that treasure...is purpose.

The Intimate Truth of Treasure

When you begin to live out intimacy with the King, you realize the deeper meaning of the parable of Matthew 13. You realize that Jesus isn't only talking about the treasure as a far-off Kingdom. Instead, you realize that to the Bridegroom, *it is His bride that is the treasure*. God's children are His treasure. And it is HE who offered everything to take possession of that treasure.

And this means that *you are the gold*. But it's not just you. His treasure is also *everyone* else in this world that He loves. And Jesus didn't just purchase a great treasure that only moves into full maturity when it dies. He wasn't buying investment property! He bought a treasure that has its full worth and value right now. In other words, the Kingdom of Heaven isn't a place we go to when we die. We are part of the Kingdom of Heaven NOW.

And when you know this, when you receive this, and when it sits in your heart ... all of a sudden, you want everyone else to know their true value as well. You can't help it. Love Himself compels you. You begin to see treasure all around you.

Because it's not just about finding and recognizing treasure - it's about how we reveal it.

The Revealing

It doesn't take a person of God to point out the trash in someone or what they do wrong. The world does that every day. And it is super easy to make judgments based on someone's mistakes.

And we all do it. We are programmed for it.

And to prove this, I want to show you a picture.

 This photo of me, which was designed to look as if it was a candid photo of me deep in thought, was taken while filming a documentary series that's a companion piece to this book in your hand.

But here's the thing about that photo. Look deep. Because this photo was part of a social experiment that we filmed to highlight how our judgment of others' shortcomings colors our thoughts and perceptions.

You undoubtedly noticed the mathematical formulas, and I'm sure a major glaring error jumped off the page at you. After all, we learn in kindergarten that 5 + 5 equals 10, not 13. It is obvious. My 5-year-old can point that out.

But as part of this thought experiment we filmed, I posted this photo on social media to see the response to this mistake and how it would be commented on.

And unfortunately, the predictable happened.

My feed lit up like fireworks on the Fourth of July!

Nearly every other comment on the photo was about the incorrect formula. Some of the comment threads devolved quickly with folks making jokes about how people where I live in the UK apparently don't know simple math. Others laughed at me for looking so serious in front of a simple mistake. There were plenty of folks getting in a joke at my expense, and people made judgment calls on me - I've sloppy arithmetic, inattentive to detail, and some called me just plain old dumb.

If I were offendable, it would have stung.

But not a single person, not one, paid attention to the *correct* formulas, including the theoretical formula directly behind me – the quantum computations for Creation, *thus giving the reasoning for God*!

But no.

Every critical comment focused on what I got wrong, and no one commented on what I got right. Everyone zeroed in on where they believed I fell short. There were people even demonstrating their unconscious superiority – *I* *would have never done this or that, *I* was taught math in school, unlike this guy*, that sort of thing. And people loved to pile on. My social media feed for this photo was full of laughing emojis.

But in focusing on the mistake, everyone looking at the photo missed the next-level stuff going on next to it, which was correct.

And while this was an intentional and simple arithmetic mistake, the response to it is a great example of what the RELIGIOUS MINDSET causes us to do. The religious spirit causes us to make judgments where we think people fall short and make mistakes, and to elevate ourselves because of it. And our judgments devalue others based on their perceived errors and shortcomings.

But here's the thing. Short of Jesus, we can never measure up to what He deserves from us. He is holy and beautiful, the Creator of the universe. But our failings and shortcomings do not make us less valuable to Him. And no matter what you have done, it cannot diminish your worth in His eyes. And when we understand that and partner with Jesus to call out this treasure in others, it's not to point out where others are wrong but to reveal the gold and purpose that Jesus put inside of them before time began.

Translating the Treasure Map

Now let's take a pause and take a breath. I want you to understand the weight of this moment because this is a very difficult pill to swallow.

You are a treasure. And at this point in your journey, I know you can comprehend this.

But what is harder to digest, is that Jesus also considers your neighbor who may be cheating on her husband a treasure. The son who steals from his family, spits on his legacy, and then leaves them behind is a treasure. Those in prison guilty of committing the most heinous crimes, to Jesus, are a treasure.

And the people who have hurt you deepest are also a treasure.

I know it's not easy to read. It's not easy for me to write. If you have any inkling of my life, you know that almost everything inside me is screaming and rebelling against this truth.

It's not fair! It's not right!

Right now, everything in my conscious body is battling me and taking me to task. And I know that you may be going through the same. I know you may have been hurt in unimaginable ways by people you trusted. Words cannot describe the anguish you have gone through, maybe even are experiencing right now. Wounds from people you trusted, people that you believed in, those who promised never to hurt you. And yet they did. Over and over, they did, leaving you in desperate pain.

It's *not* fair. It's *not* right.

But it is the Father's will *to see none perish, but all come to repentance* (2 Peter 3:9).

When Jesus cried out, *Father forgive them, they know now what they do*, He wasn't referring to just His mother, His most loved disciple, or Mary Magdalene who were watching in the crowd. He was talking about those that cheered his crucifixion. He was crying out for the Roman soldiers who had flayed the flesh from his bones. He was petitioning the Father for the one who shoved the crown of thorns down onto his head, splitting his skin apart like shredded paper. He desired forgiveness for the centurions who cast lots for His garments as He hung naked and exposed on the rough-hewn cross. He was crying out for the Pharisees and Sadducees who connived and manipulated to have him murdered. He was crying out for Pilate who authorized His execution.

Jesus asked the Father to forgive them. And He died for them too.

Are you beginning to understand the cost of great treasure?

When confronted with the weight of this reality, our first instinct is to say, *Yes, Jesus loves and forgives them. But...*

And let me stop you right there. There is no BUT. Just as there is no BUT for you, and there is no BUT for me. Thank God.

This recognition of someone's value in Christ does not mean that those who have hurt us are allowed access to us again. Nor should they receive it. And this doesn't mean what they did was right. Because it was not justifiable. But it does mean that if we are to live out the truth that Christ lives in us and we live in Him, then we must move from *His* reality first. We must see those who have hurt us, even in the deepest of ways, as loved by their Creator.

And, yes, there IS a time and a place for correction. Mistakes DO need to be brought into the light. After all, as the author of the Book of James says, we are *to confess our sins to one another* (James 5:16), and what is done in the darkness will be exposed.

But what often happens is that when we have been wronged, we begin to see ourselves as superior to others. And soon thereafter, self-right-eousness creeps in. And correcting others from a place of "perceived" superiority when either there is no real relationship or when there is a broken relationship, will always come across as an attack. Always. This is why critical debates on social media are so often destined for failure, no matter how much logic and research are poured into different respons-es. Firm correction outside of a relationship is destined for failure.

No matter our intent.

It's the Holy Spirit that convicts the world of its errors. Not me. And not you. And we never get to judge someone because they sin different-ly than we do, even when that sin is directed against us. This is why megaphone street preachers, who tell people how awful and evil they are, are completely ineffective. This is why pastors who throw out cruel missives from their pulpits in their Sunday sermons are losing those they are called to shepherd.

We have to ask the question, what was it about Jesus?

What was it about Jesus that pulled the immoral and the sinful to Him?

What was it that made them feel safe with Him?

And not only that but when they came into Jesus' orbit, what was it about Jesus that left these people *forever changed?* The religious leaders despised Jesus for this. They could not stand that a man claimed to know and speak with God and dined with those they considered less than. The authorities could not believe such a man could work miracles and speak into people's hearts. And they loathed the fact that people were seeking Jesus out instead of them, and after these people met Jesus, they were radically changed because of it.

Jesus didn't coddle those who came to Him. He could be firm, confrontational even. But every word from His mouth resonated with the love of the Father so that even His admonishments dripped with invitations to know God deeper.

Many modern believers are too comfortable using fear, shame, superiority, and anger as motivators to try to force or guilt someone into the kingdom of God. In essence, we try to use negative force to establish a positive reaction. But that doesn't reveal treasure. It only plants bad seeds. And rotten seed only produces rotten fruit. This is what Jesus meant in Matthew 23:15 when He said, *What sorrow awaits you teachers of religious law and you Pharisees. Hypocrites! For you cross land and sea to make one convert, and then you turn that person into twice the child of hell you yourselves are!*

But love never fails. And when we know the truth, that He is the treasure and that we are the treasure, we are compelled to find the gold in others. Suddenly, we're not seeing people through their mistakes, BUT THROUGH THEIR WORTH.

We are called to be witnesses to Christ's glory through our love, not our judgment.

We are called to enter into relationship with one another. To love one another. To disciple others and bring them into this INTIMATE DANCE with the one who loved us first. This is how true radical change happens in people's lives. And this is how real salvation comes. And this is the Kingdom of Heaven breaking through into a person's life *now*.

This is the discovery of the treasure of the Kingdom.

Discovering Treasure in the Most Unlikely of Places

Do you mind if I tell you a personal story of finding treasure in the wildest place you can imagine?

On the ground in Cuba (and with much more hair!)

Years ago, I was in Cuba on a short-term trip, and witchcraft is a huge deal in this country. Villages are filled with practitioners of the old ways. And I'm going to be painfully honest here, most people there are more trusting of their ancestral customs than the institutional Church.

The village I spent most of my time in was in the shadow of a large mountain, and at the top of this mountain lived a powerful family – Santerian priests that had reigned over the mountains for generations through their ancestral magic.

For years, visiting Christian missionaries had made a practice of venturing up that mountain looking for a fight. They'd march their groups to the witches' property line, and the Christians would rebuke them, call down God's fire, Jericho march around their land, try to cast devils out ... you know, all the stuff.

These missionaries were looking for their Elijah moment, where they could prove that their God was greater than those the witches prayed to. In return, the family of witches would hurl curses back, do rituals, and cast spells. Stories abounded of people who had traveled up the mountain to confront this generational line of witches and would soon fall ill, run into money troubles, or run into misfortune after misfortune. It wasn't a good scene for anyone, and there definitely wasn't any good fruit coming from these tense interchanges. The only fruit blooming was bucketloads of anger and fear all around.

So, when my host told me the stories and asked if I wanted to journey up the mountain to "pray for the witches," I jumped at the chance.

The next morning, before our journey, I began to pray to Papa for a breakthrough with this family, for them to know His love, for their hearts to be softened, and for them to "respond." I asked the Lord for access to their hearts – you know, so they could be "saved" and know His Glory.

I mean, that sounds all well and good, doesn't it? That's a wonderful agenda to pray for, right?

But then the Bridegroom said something that wrecked me. While praying, I heard Jesus explicitly say, *Ken, I will NOT give you access to their hearts. NOT UNTIL YOU'RE WILLING TO LOVE THEM AS I DO.*

And I was shattered with realization.

You see, my prayers, which I thought were good and well-intentioned, reeked of manipulation. And when I held my prayers up to the love of Jesus, I found that I was "loving" this family from an agenda – trying to "save" them. A noble thing, yes, but I was praying for them as if they were *a target*, something to be conquered.

Basically, *I* was resorting to a form of witchcraft to try and prove the Glory of the Lord and "save" the witches.

And I had left TRUE love out of it.

The Lord reminded me of the parable of the woman and her lost coin –

Or suppose a woman has 10 silver coins and loses 1. Doesn't she light a lamp, sweep the house and search carefully until she finds it? And when she finds it, she calls her friends and neighbors together and says, 'Rejoice with me; I have found my lost coin.' In the same way, I tell you, there is rejoicing in the presence of the angels of God over one sinner who repents.
-Luke 15:8-10

Now the symbology in this parable is amazing, and I recommend re-searching it. Still, I want to stick to the major point the Lord brought me to – although the coin was lost, the coin *still* belonged to its owner, and the coin *never* lost its original value. Even though the coin was hidden under dirt, maybe even unrecognizable, it still held its original worth to the person searching for it.

Then Jesus nudged me with ANOTHER parable we all know, The Prodigal Son. In the story, a father's son demands his inheritance, abandons his family, squanders his fortune, and ends up on the bad side of a famine. Desperate, the son goes home to beg his father's forgiveness with the intent to work for him as a slave. But before the son can even get the words out of his mouth, the father restores the son's position, authority, and status in the family and community and covers him with LOVE ... because, to the Father, the son was ALWAYS a son. The son may have been lost for a time, but to the father, the son was a son and would always be a son.

The lost son was the father's true fortune. The son was the father's treasure.

And just like that, everything changed for me.

I didn't have to go confront these witches to challenge them or rebuke them. I didn't need to call down fire. I needed to remember what Spirit I was of – *that of a Savior's love*

I didn't need a *call down fire* Elijah moment. I needed a *release the love of Jesus* moment.

And I can't save anyone. Only Jesus' love redeems.

And then God allowed me to see from the witches' perspective - how they had been treated by Christians. My heart broke as I realized their only experience with Christians was the farthest thing from LOVE one can imagine. All they knew of Christians was outrage, judgment, and condemnation. And in return, they were scared, angry, and fearful. Of course they acted negatively! Wouldn't you?

And here's something else. God is CRAZY protective in ways we don't realize. The Gospels are chock full of stories of Jesus protecting people from the religious spirit that sought to twist God's love and intent, and thought to control access to His love.

And I realized that God had been protecting these witches *from Christians* who weren't carrying the Lord's heart for them. And He had been waiting for this moment to reveal Himself through someone willing to carry the lamp oil of His love.

In the revealing of treasure, God's heart is about reconciling the world to Himself through Christ. And He has given us the pleasure of this ministry-

> *Or do you have contempt for the treasure of his kindness, forbearance, and patience, and yet do not know that God's kindness leads you to repentance -Romans 2:4*

That family wasn't a box to be checked. They weren't a variable in an evangelism growth chart. They weren't a number in a quarterly report. And they weren't a family to be spiritually conquered.

In the Father's eyes, that family was a treasure. He already knew them. He already loved them. And He already knew where they were in their hearts.

I just had to show up and be his ambassador.

I charged up that mountain path on Cloud Nine, envisioning these witches as people that were so cherished and valued by God, that I was literally infused with His love.

We walked right up to the house's front door and knocked, and a woman about 40 years old greeted us. She wasn't wearing robes or carrying a wizard's staff. And she wasn't bathed in blood. She looked like someone you pass on the street daily or find walking the aisles of Wal-Mart or Target.

My friend introduced us, and I immediately asked if I could bless her home.

And then I asked if I could give her a hug.

And crazy enough, she obliged.

When I wrapped my arms around her, I felt the love of Jesus surge out of every pore of my body, flooding into the door of her home, quieting the darkness, anger, and fear. I felt like I was hugging a long-lost friend, and we had known each other forever. Tears burst from my eyes. And when we finally broke our embrace, tears were running down her cheeks, as well. Looking back, I can confidently say that hug was one of the best hugs of my life. And all I can say is that it was Jesus.

The priestess invited us into her home and introduced me to her husband, the Babalawo of the mountain. The look of shock on his face was priceless, and the cowrie shells in his hand for a divination ritual dropped to the ground with a clink. Before he had a chance to recover, I walked over to him and took his hand in mine, greeting him as a brother and telling him I had merely come to bless his home.

And for the next five hours, we sat in the simple home of this family that everyone had been so terrified of, surrounded by tools of ritual magic, skulls, and animal bones. We drank tea while watching the sunset over the mountainside, talking about life, love, and Jesus.

Looking at them, I didn't see a priest and priestess of the armies of darkness to be beaten in a spiritual battle. I didn't care about the rumors of curses. All I could see was the treasure that this family was in God's eyes, the gold that they had in their hearts - gold that God put there, before time began, just waiting to be uncovered.

I saw a family God loved so much that He sent His only Son.

I told them who God said they were, how much they were loved, and how they were a treasure. I asked for their forgiveness for those who had come before, who moved with good intent but with improper application. And then I prayed for Jesus to bless them, heal them, and protect their home from those who sought to harm them.

The priestess asked if she could know the Spirit I carried. She said that the spirits she worked with had abandoned her as soon as we had hugged, and she knew then she had to invite me in. She said all she could feel was the Spirit that entered with me, its warmth and love, and she wanted that Spirit to stay.

And then I informed her that if the Spirit that came with me stayed, the other spirits she prayed to could never return.

Distraught, she said it was impossible for her to stop working with her spirits. Her ancestors had worked with these powerful forces for generations. Leaving her *orishas* would mean rejecting her entire family's history and breaking covenants. It was who she was. It was her identity. She just kept saying *It's imposible', it's imposible'* repeatedly while wringing her hands.

But then a voice whispered in my ear, and I told her what the Voice said- *With men this is impossible, but with God all things are possible* (Matt 19:26).

That fated meeting was six years ago.

And now?

That family that everyone was so terrified of are now radical lovers of Jesus. And they spread His love to any who will receive it. They find gold in the unlikeliest of places. And they call out the truth of who people are in God's sight. They are local missionaries, spreading the truth of God's love throughout the mountains of their ancestral home. They pray for those who were once like them, the witches the Christians tried to pick fights with. And through love, they are changing the face of a nation, finding lost coins wherever they go.

Love, after all, never fails.

Embrace the Hunt

Your purpose is to be loved, and to be a witness to Christ's glory through that love. To know you are a treasure, and to reveal treasure in others.

When you're in love, everyone knows. And those in love, help others fall in love.

Because treasure hunters create treasure hunters.

We are called to enter into relationship with one another. To love one another. To disciple others and bring them into this intimate dance with the One who loved us first. This is how true change happens in people's lives.

We don't draw people closer by telling them where they are wrong and by discrediting their closely held beliefs. It's not about supernatural showdowns and picking fights. It's about shining so bright with His love that His majesty cannot be denied, of shining so spectacularly that those who see it can't help but ask, *How do I know the source of your love?*

That is how you become the light that everyone flocks to:

You are the light of the world. A city that is set on a hill cannot be hidden. Nor do they light a lamp and put it under a basket, but on a lampstand, and it gives light to all who are in the house Matthew 5:14-15

The search for treasure is about the love of Christ shining through you, disarming the powers and authorities through the love offered from the cross and resurrection.

It's about revealing the gold. Gold that God put there for others to find.

You're a treasure hunter, you see.

It's what you do by being who you are – passionately loved by your Creator. And in the realm of His divine love, we are invited to embark on a sacred quest for the hidden treasures within each soul. It is through this journey that we can reveal the intimate love of God, as we venture into the depths of the human experience through the lens of His passion and desire.

Just as a treasure hunter embarks on an expedition to unearth precious gems and jewels, we are called to seek out the hidden riches within each person. These treasures - often obscured by the complexities of life, by our judgments, and our pains - can only be discovered through the gaze of His pure love.

We're invited to embrace the mystery of the human heart, recognizing that every individual holds a unique treasure waiting to be unveiled. Through compassionate understanding and genuine connection, we can navigate the intricate labyrinth of emotions, fears, and vulnerabilities, gently revealing the truth of each person's being.

And as we venture deeper into the realms of the heart, we come to understand that the true treasure lies not only within ourselves but also in recognition of the divine spark present in others. Through acts of kindness, empathy, and acceptance, we honor the sacredness of each individual, illuminating the path to intimacy and love.

It is in this sacred dance of seeking and revealing that the intimate love of God comes alive. As we recognize and appreciate the inherent beauty within every soul, we become full vessels of His love, emanating its transformative and glorious power into the world.

We are here to embark on this journey together, embracing the mystery of the intimate love of God. And as we dare to delve into the depths of His love, let us unveil the hidden treasures within ourselves and others, igniting connections that transcend the boundaries of space and time.

We have been given the sacred quest of being treasure hunters. And through this quest, may we reveal the transformative power of God's Divine love, bringing forth a world where the treasures of the human heart shine brightly for all to behold.

Scripture References

Matthew 5:14-15 - "You are the light of the world. A city built on a hill cannot be hid. No one after lighting a lamp puts it under the bushel basket, but on the lampstand, and it gives light to all in the house."

Matthew 13:44-45 - "The kingdom of heaven is like treasure hidden in a field, which someone found and hid; then in his joy he goes and sells all that he has and buys that field. Again, the kingdom of heaven is like a merchant in search of fine pearls; on finding one pearl of great value, he went and sold all that he had and bought it."

Matthew 19:26 - "But Jesus looked at them and said, 'For mortals it is impossible, but for God all things are possible.'"

Matthew 22:37-39 - "He said to him, 'You shall love the Lord your God with all your heart, and with all your soul, and with all your mind.' This is the greatest and first commandment. And a second is like it: 'You shall love your neighbor as yourself.'"

Matthew 23:15 - "Woe to you, scribes and Pharisees, hypocrites! For you cross sea and land to make a single convert, and you make the new convert twice as much a child of hell as yourselves."

Luke 15:8-10 - "Or what woman having ten silver coins, if she loses one of them, does not light a lamp, sweep the house, and search carefully until she finds it? When she has found it, she calls together her friends and neighbors, saying, 'Rejoice with me, for I have found the coin that I had lost.' Just so, I tell you, there is joy in the presence of the angels of God over one sinner who repents."

Luke 15:11-32 – "Then Jesus said, 'There was a man who had two sons. The younger of them said to his father, "Father, give me the share of the property that will belong to me." So he divided his property between them. A few days later the younger son gathered all he had and traveled to a distant country, and there he squandered his property in dissolute living. When he had spent everything, a severe famine took place throughout that country, and he began to be in need. So he went and hired himself out to one of the citizens of that country, who sent him to his fields to feed the pigs. He would gladly have filled himself with the pods that the pigs were eating; and no one gave him anything. But when he came to himself he said, "How many of my father's hired hands have bread enough and to spare, but here I am dying of hunger! I will get up and go to my father, and I will say to him, 'Father, I have sinned against heaven and before you; I am no longer worthy to be called your son; treat me like one of your hired hands.'" So he set off and went to his father. But while he was still far off, his father saw him and was filled with compassion; he ran and put his arms around him and kissed him. Then the son said to him, "Father, I have sinned against heaven and before you; I am no longer worthy to be called your son." But the father said to his slaves, "Quickly, bring out a robe—the best one—and put it on him; put a ring on his finger and sandals on his feet. And get the fatted calf and kill it, and let us eat and celebrate; for this son of mine was dead and is alive again; he was lost and is found!" And they began to celebrate.'"

Luke 23:34 - "Then Jesus said, 'Father, forgive them; for they do not know what they are doing.' And they cast lots to divide his clothes."

John 3:16 - "For God so loved the world that he gave his only Son, so that everyone who believes in him may not perish but may have eternal life."

John 13:34 - "I give you a new commandment, that you love one another. Just as I have loved you, you also should love one another."

Acts 16:25 - "About midnight Paul and Silas were praying and singing hymns to God, and the prisoners were listening to them."

Romans 2:4 - "Or do you despise the riches of his kindness and forbearance and patience? Do you not realize that God's kindness is meant to lead you to repentance?"

Romans 3:23 - "since all have sinned and fall short of the glory of God."

Romans 5:8 - "But God proves his love for us in that while we still were sinners Christ died for us."

Romans 12:19 - "Beloved, never avenge yourselves, but leave room for the wrath of God; for it is written, 'Vengeance is mine, I will repay, says the Lord.'"

1 Corinthians 6:19-20 - "Or do you not know that your body is a temple of the Holy Spirit within you, which you have from God, and that you are not your own? For you were bought with a price; therefore glorify God in your body."

1 Corinthians 13:4-7 - "Love is patient; love is kind; love is not envious or boastful or arrogant or rude. It does not insist on its own way; it is not irritable or resentful; it does not rejoice in wrongdoing but rejoices in the truth. It bears all things, believes all things, hopes all things, endures all things."

2 Corinthians 5:17 - "So if anyone is in Christ, there is a new creation: everything old has passed away; see, everything has become new!"

Ephesians 4:2-3 - "With all humility and gentleness, with patience, bearing with one another in love, making every effort to maintain the unity of the Spirit in the bond of peace."

Galatians 5:22-23 - "But the fruit of the Spirit is love, joy, peace, patience, kindness, goodness, faithfulness, gentleness, and self-control. There is no law against such things."

James 5:16 - "Therefore confess your sins to one another, and pray for one another, so that you may be healed. The prayer of the righteous is powerful and effective."

1 Peter 4:8 - "Above all, maintain constant love for one another, for love covers a multitude of sins."

2 Peter 3:9 - "The Lord is not slow about his promise, as some think of slowness, but is patient with you, not wanting any to perish, but all to come to repentance."

Notes

Initial
_____
_____
_____
_____
_____
_____
_____
_____
_____
_____
_____
_____

Later
_____
_____
_____
_____
_____

REVELATION SEVEN

REVOLUTION

W e've come so far together.

But you have only just begun.

In the multi-faceted realms of God's beautiful mysteries, His invitation beckons us to embark on a continual journey of joining in union with the love of Christ. And it's within this sacred union that the essence of Christianity takes on a profound and transformative meaning, calling us to reimagine our understanding of faith.

After experiencing God intimately, when pushing past the rent veil, can you go back to life as usual? Will the standard Christian activities do it for you? Are Sunday morning services the ultimate end all be all now? Were they ever? Are they still *gamedays,* as so many churches' "check the box" leadership programs like to call them?

Or is your walk with God now so much more?

His love defies easy human comprehension. There is nothing wrong with the normal Christian activities – church on Sunday morning, small group on Wednesday, maybe a prayer meeting in the mornings. But *being* with Him is so much more. And so much more tangible. It is through this union with Christ, the embodiment of divine love, that we are invited to venture beyond the boundaries of conventional Christianity and explore the limitless depths of spiritual connection. For when you are in love, truly in love, your thoughts always fall upon the object of your affection.

And His thoughts are constantly upon you.

The allure of His love entices us to go beyond mere religious doctrines and rituals. It compels us to embrace profound transformation, where the barriers of separation have been torn from top to bottom, and we become one with the God who is not just responsible for all of creation, but who is in love with His creation.

This union with the divine love of Christ unveils a reality beyond words—a sacred communion that transcends human limitations. It draws us into the depths of our bodies and our souls, and through our Spirit where we are seated in Christ - where the mysterious dance between the human and the divine takes place.

And as we surrender, we are invited to reimagine what being a Christian truly means. It transcends dogma, doctrine, and external practices, unveiling a path of inner transformation and spiritual awakening. It calls us to embody the teachings of Christ, not merely as a historical figure, but as a living Presence, THE living Presence within our hearts and souls.

Through this intimate encounter, Christianity becomes more than a simple journey of personal transformation. It becomes an awakening to the true reality beyond the matrix of fabricated reality the world has hoisted upon us from birth. It invites us to embody the unconditional love, compassion, and grace that Christ exemplified, transcending the confines of religious boundaries and embracing the universal essence of His love.

In the deep places of this union, we realize that Christianity is not confined to the walls of institutions but expands into the fabric of our every moment. It becomes a way of being—a transformative path that embraces the sacred mysteries of love and invites us to co-create a world infused with compassion, unity, and peace, coming together where we agree – JESUS – instead of dividing upon religious, political, and categorical lines.

As we venture deeper into embracing Christ's divine love, we reawaken to the beauty of our interconnectedness and our inherent divinity. For we are designed to reign with Him *who loved us and washed us from our sins in His own blood, and has made us kings and priests to His God and Father, to Him be glory and dominion forever and ever* (Revelation 1:5-6). And it is through this union with Jesus that Christianity unfolds as a journey of intimacy, an invitation to embody the profound mystery of divine love and radiate its transformative power into the world.

And the world has gotten tastes of this reality in fleeting moments that seem to kiss the Earth but then move on. There's even a term that people have used to attempt to define it. It's a word both spoken from the pulpits of the powerful and invoked by the unknown in their quiet prayer rooms. It is sung about, written of, searched out, prophesied, and in some cases, attempts have been made to manufacture it. Entire schools, universities, and worldwide ministries have been created to usher it in, enable it, and sustain it. And it is a word that quickens the pulse of believers worldwide, met with cheers and longing...

Revival!

But what exactly is Revival? Is it an event, a movement, or something else? Can Revival be planned and organized?

Can you even find the word Revival in the Scriptures?

And what does the word Revival mean for those on an intimate Journey with Jesus?

And what if … just what if … *we are called to more?*

But, What IS Revival?

It may shock you, but there is NO mention of the word 'Revival' in the Bible.

Jesus never used the word. Neither did the apostles.

Yes, 11 verses in the Old Testament mention REVIVING, but in the way that we have been taught about REVIVAL, the word doesn't exist in the Scriptures. If you were to ask a Jewish person where you could find the word REVIVAL in the Tanakh, they would have no idea what you were talking about. And this is because Revival is not a Biblical term. It's a church term. It's a part of our special language – Christianese – if you will. And the word didn't even come into use until the 18th century.

Now, just because Revival isn't mentioned in the Bible, it doesn't mean it is not real. The Magna Carta wasn't mentioned in the Bible, South America wasn't mentioned, and neither were cell phones and televisions. The United States wasn't mentioned in the Bible either.

Yet these things are very real.

I believe wholeheartedly in Revival. Revival is as much of a real thing as other Church history terms such as Reformation, Protestantism, Catholicism, Denominationalism, and a whole bunch of other *-isms*.

Revival is very real. And it is wonderful.

But Revival was never something we were told to specifically pray for by Jesus or by any author of the books of the New Testament. It is not something we specifically were told to plan or organize or judge good results by. And maybe more importantly, Revival is not something we are supposed to pray toward as if it is the ultimate end all be all. Because the truth is, it is not. Revival is not the ultimate final boss level of faith awesomeness.

And Revival is for sure, absolutely, unequivocally, not something that we are supposed to idolize and put up on a pedestal – which is what we tend to do. And it's where we go off course.

Point blank, I'm not called to yearn for Revival.

I am called to yearn for Jesus.

When looking back at the largest world-altering Revival movement of the past two centuries, The Welsh Revival, at the center of this Revival were people pursuing relationships of pure abandon with the King at any cost. They weren't trying to sell tickets to events, sell more books, or prop up churches whose memberships were dwindling. They were men and women who dared to believe that God was who He said He was and that God was still desiring a connection with His children and revealing Himself to the world.

Seth & Frank Joshua

Imagine the courage of men like the Joshua brothers in the dawn of the 20th century in Wales, men whose hearts were so ablaze with the boundless compassion of Jesus that they found themselves compelled to sing with unyielding faith outside the brothels and the train station of the rugged mining town of Neath. They were emissaries of God's love, standing firm in the face of mockery and scorn, assuring every soul that they were cherished deeply by God.

Consider the audacious spirit of young women like Florrie Evans, who, when societal norms demanded silence, rose to her feet in a large church gathering and filled with the Spirit, declaring with unshakeable conviction, *"I love the Lord Jesus Christ with all my heart."* Her words, so potent and sincere, drove people to their knees, stirring within them a profound awakening of faith.

And then there were individuals like Evan Roberts, a humble miner from the shadowy coal pits of Wales, in training to be a pastor. His devotion was such that he spent countless hours in communion with God in the Secret Place, transforming himself into a conduit for the love of Jesus. His prayer, *"Bend me, oh Lord, bend me,"* ignited the spark of Revival in a small, rugged country that would surge across borders, spreading like wildfire across the entire world.

Evan Roberts

These were people of faith and spirit. They were ordinary men and women who, with their yearning love for Jesus, played extraordinary roles in the history of the Christian faith. In the dark and rain of Wales, they became the beacon of God's love, illuminating the world with the radiance of faith, hope, and divine love like bright, shining cities on a hill.

Because they understood real Revival is not an event.

Real Revival is your dry bones coming alive in intimacy with the Holy Spirit.

Real Revival is the destruction of your false identity and you waking up to the reality of who you are – a child of God.

Real Revival is knowing who your Father is – a loving Creator who designed you to create with Him and would stop at nothing to destroy every barrier between you and Him.

Real Revival is you realizing who Jesus is – the Bridegroom who intimately desires His bride, and for you to know Him as He knows you.

Real Revival is you becoming a Thin Place, where multiple dimensions and reality collide, making you an atmosphere changer, a releaser of His Glory and Presence so that His love and passion flow out of you like a river of Living Water.

Real Revival comes from you dwelling in the Secret Place, entering into the Bridal Chamber, and becoming united with God.

Real Revival is becoming so overwhelmed with His love, that you realize that He is the treasure, and you are the treasure, as well as everyone He loves.

And real Revival is entering into the wonder that He IS and reveling in the expectation of the Holy Spirit's freeing power in every area of life.

Real Revival comes to regions when His children stand collectively and say, *"Lord, we will do whatever it takes to reveal your Glory to those who will receive it."*

And *mass* Revival is the result of singular men and women, just like YOU, fully powered by intimacy with Jesus, filled with that yearning and intimacy catching fire and spreading throughout all who witness it.

Because He is God. And He is worthy.

The Yearning

The problem with our current understanding of Revival is that we believe it is an event. We believe it is a movement. We place Revival upon a pedestal and yearn for it, more than we yearn for the King. But when we call out for Revival more than yearning for intimacy, we are missing something important – Revival can be asked for, and it can be proclaimed ... but outside of intimacy with Jesus, it's nothing. It's just another meeting, or a conference designed to sell tickets and books. And sure, some good things may come of these larger meetings, but in the end, these types of Revivals are not true transformations, and they're definitely not the revelation of God's glory.

And outside of intimacy with God, Revival cannot be sustained.

Because God's version of Revival is so much more than what we understand.

History shows us that once people with true intimacy with the Lord release real Revival, once the miracles begin and the fires start flowing, some predictable things happen.

First, we try to make a plan. Then we try to organize and quantify our results. And then, we try to build a system around the Revival to continue seeing results.

In other words, we attempt to institute control.

And soon, we begin to rely on the manipulation of emotional responses to gauge our success – how many people raise their hands or attend our events, instead of how many people actually enter into a relationship with the King and live transformed lives.

But here's the thing. If it's not intimacy, it's not a true transformation – it's not a renewal of the heart and mind. It's not real salvation.

And once the Revival becomes about anything more than a by-product of intimacy with the King, it begins its swift end. Because Revival is not supposed to be the end result.

It's supposed to be a new beginning.

The Renewal and Restoration

Maybe, it is time we change our understanding of Revival.

Our understanding of Revival is focused on resuscitating the old. Revival comes from the word revive, as in, revive something that has fallen ill or lifeless. So that means Revival, as it is often reflected in the Church, is actually about resuscitating old wineskins. And Jesus had something to say about this in Luke 5:36-39:

> *And no one puts new wine into old wineskins; otherwise the new wine will burst the skins and will be spilled, and the skins will be destroyed. But new wine must be put into fresh wineskins. And no one after drinking old wine desires new wine, but says, 'The old is good. '*

When God revives us, He calls us into a new reality. When He shakes off dry bones, He's not wanting to go back to the way things used to be.

When Ezekiel spoke to the dry bones in Ezekiel 37, old flesh didn't form on the bones. God created new flesh upon them. When Jesus created 120 gallons of wine from water in John 2, He didn't create a wine that was the same as before or of lesser quality. No, Jesus created the best wine available! When we enter into a truly intimate relationship with Jesus, Paul calls us a *kainos creation*, meaning of a new kind, unprecedented, novel, uncommon, unheard-of creation!

This is REAL Revival - becoming who God called you to be before the beginning of time, fully realized through your intimate journey with Him!

God's type of Revival is intended to lead us into something we've never seen before, and most importantly, once seen, we cannot EVER go back to life as usual!

God's version of Revival is what happened 3,000 years ago when a young boy loved God so much that he could not stop singing his praises while he was in the fields tending his father's sheep. And when that young boy became a king, that king would go on to bring about worship to God on a scale that was never before seen in human history. That young shepherd boy pulled a Heavenly reality into the Earthly realm. All because a little boy loved God so much, and grew so intimate with Him, that he would grow to be called a man after God's own heart! And Israel would not, could not, ever be the same.

But not only did King David bring about the reality of worship to God to the kingdom of Israel, but those praises of when he was but a little boy in an arid field would seed the very soil with his intimacy. And those fields 1000 years later would become the outskirts of a small town called Bethlehem, becoming the very place God would be born into flesh!

God's Revival is how the disciples could not go back to "normal life" after witnessing Jesus post-resurrection. John 21 shows us that professional fishermen couldn't even catch fish anymore, for the Lord had called them to be fishers of men. These individual men who intimately knew Jesus could never go back to life as it was, and they answered the call, bringing the Gospel to the corners of the known world! There was no going back!

Life could never go back to being the same!

The Cost of Intimacy

Now that we are near the end of your new beginning, the question must be asked.

Do you really want God's version of Revival?

Yes, it sounds wonderful, doesn't it? A transformed life. Living your true identity. Stepping into the reality of who God says you are.

But it comes with a price.

Yes, it sounds wonderful that during the Welsh Revival the jails and courts were empty, the bars and pubs were bare, all the alcohol had to be poured out, and the churches were full all hours of the day with people quitting their jobs to attend wild worship services.

But one of the little reported facts of the Welsh Revival is that it crashed local economies. Restaurants, pubs, government offices, theatres, and police officers had no revenue. Society was upended!

If Revival actually struck, would you leave your job? Would you follow the passion of the Lord wherever, and whenever, it took you? What if your employer got wrapped up in Kingdom Power and sold the business you work for, leaving you out of a job? What if the housing market crashed because the economy became unhinged? What if the economy completely tanked, drying up your 401K and your life savings?

Are you willing to leave it all behind? Is intimacy with God still worth it?

Are you willing to sacrifice everything for Him, just like the heroes of the Welsh Revival did? Are you willing to put your life on the line, as the saints of old? Would you sacrifice everything, just as Jesus did, when He placed his hands down to have spikes hammered into them?

Are you one who is truly willing to bend?

What if God's version of Revival doesn't look like you expect it to?

What if God's next Revival isn't in the church buildings, but is in the country fields and city streets? What if God's next cadre of leaders and emissaries aren't clergy or folks with seminary degrees, but instead were addicts, prostitutes, or former Satan worshipers who had a real encounter with the King and could not stop talking about His goodness and mercy, who ran into the towns and city centers to proclaim the goodness of God without the benefit of reading books on Systematic Theology?

Are you willing to leave your idea of what the Church should look like behind?

What if the next major move of God didn't come from the platform, the stage, or from those behind the camera, but instead came from the least among us, from the broken, the meek, the used - those who had seen the face of the King and were so consumed with His love, that it infected everyone around them and made them say *Bend me, oh Lord. Bend me.*

Because God's version of Revival is so much more than slapping the name Revival on a flier or social media post. When God's version of Revival comes, life, as usual, is over.

Because while we clamor for Revival and transformation, what God is calling us to is REVOLUTION.

Revolution Calling

Funny thing about Revival. People pray for it. Pastors call out for it. Congregations ask God to bring it.

But Revival isn't God's responsibility to release.

It's ours.

We can pray for God to bring Revival all day long. But the truth is, God is waiting for us. He has already given us Revival – His Son. And God's glory fills the earth; it has never left!

When we cry out for Revival, we cry out for something God has already given us. But it is something we do not know how to access intimately. It surrounds us. It is all around us, literally permeating the atmospheres of our homes, our towns, and cities. It covers the earth, as the waters cover the seas. We are constantly surrounded by His Glory, which is the love of Jesus. What is lacking is our awareness of this intimate love, right there, within our grasp.

Your Father is waiting for you to step into Revolution.

Your Father is waiting for you to rise and release His love wherever you go, to pull from your creative heart His revolution of Glory. He is waiting for His Children to accept the responsibility and release a REVOLUTION OF LOVE wherever they tread. All creation is eagerly awaiting the revealing of the sons and daughters, those willing to stop at nothing to reveal the love of the Father.

He's waiting for those brave enough to step into their destiny, stand and say *I* will do whatever it takes. *I* love the Lord Jesus Christ with all my heart. Bend *me*.

And I'm telling you this, and I've walked with you this far to tell you that I think that person is *YOU*.

The Spirit is waiting for YOU to move.

When God violently tore the veil between realms, it wasn't so that you could add Him as a supplementary plan to improve your life. It wasn't because He wanted you to name it, claim it, and revel in prosperity as the rest of the world suffers in poverty. It was so you could know Him and know who you really are, to become an empowered Child of God designed to unleash His love within your life and to the world.

When you start walking with the God of the universe, things can never be the same. It is a revolutionary change in heart and mind. It is a revolutionary change of life as we know it from top to bottom. And like David, like the disciples, like the apostles, like the titans of the Welsh Revival, there is no going back.

When God's Revolution hits you, when you awaken to your reality as a *kainos* creation – a new species – as a son or daughter of the Most High God, life as you knew it ends.

Your identity comes from who God says YOU are, regardless of your job, your gender, your race, or whatever has been used to define you. You are a child, not a slave. Your former heart of stone hardened by the world has been ripped from you, and you have been given a new heart, bound in the Bridal Chamber to Jesus Himself.

You are included in the dance that existed since time began. As the triune God entered into a dance, creation from a spinning motion, we exist in the center of the dance of *perichoresis*, surrounded and held within the substance of God! And He has called us forth and placed us into the Dance with Him.

The Lord of the Dance has called YOU – not to meander through your life, but to dance with Him in a blaze of Glory, transforming the world around you!

YOU are a new creation, and this is your Journey. And it is one that only you can take.

The world is not the same as it was 100 years ago. The world is not the same as it was 3 years ago. And God isn't calling you to the Revival of a past time, but a Revolution in a new time. Like David, like Esther, you were made for such a time as this.

And you were born into this time for a reason.

Do you feel it? Do you feel it bubbling beneath your outstretched fingers? Do you feel the shift underneath your feet? Do you feel the tide pulling you further out?

The past days of man's Revival are about to be swarmed with God's Revolution, a revolution of men and women filled with HIS Radical love who put down their old ways and adopt the way of not only Jesus' cross, but His throne.

And it is happening now. Right now. In you.

You are designed to rule and reign with Him, co-labor, and reveal Your Father's Glory upon the earth, bring His life to everyone you know, and bring the awareness of the glory of the LORD to the earth, as the waters fill the sea.

You are a world changer. You are your Father's child.

You are a revolutionary.

This is your destiny.

And this, this revolution ... is your new beginning.

Scripture References

Psalm 42:1-2: "As a deer longs for flowing streams, so my soul longs for you, O God. My soul thirsts for God, for the living God. When shall I come and behold the face of God?"

Psalm 27:4: "One thing I asked of the Lord, that will I seek after: to live in the house of the Lord all the days of my life, to behold the beauty of the Lord, and to inquire in his temple."

Isaiah 55:6: "Seek the Lord while he may be found, call upon him while he is near."

Jeremiah 29:13: "When you search for me, you will find me; if you seek me with all your heart."

Matthew 6:6: "But whenever you pray, go into your room and shut the door and pray to your Father who is in secret; and your Father who sees in secret will reward you."

John 4:23-24: "But the hour is coming, and is now here, when the true worshipers will worship the Father in spirit and truth, for the Father seeks such as these to worship him. God is spirit, and those who worship him must worship in spirit and truth."

Acts 17:27: "so that they would search for God and perhaps grope for him and find him—though indeed he is not far from each one of us."

Ephesians 3:17-19: "and that Christ may dwell in your hearts through faith, as you are being rooted and grounded in love. I pray that you may have the power to comprehend, with all the saints, what is the breadth and length and height and depth, and to know the love of Christ that surpasses knowledge, so that you may be filled with all the fullness of God."

Colossians 1:27: "To them God chose to make known how great among the Gentiles are the riches of the glory of this mystery, which is Christ in you, the hope of glory."

Romans 12:2: "Do not be conformed to this world, but be transformed by the renewing of your minds, so that you may discern what is the will of God—what is good and acceptable and perfect."

2 Corinthians 5:17: "So if anyone is in Christ, there is a new creation: everything old has passed away; see, everything has become new!"

Revelation 3:20: "Listen! I am standing at the door, knocking; if you hear my voice and open the door, I will come in to you and eat with you, and you with me."

Ephesians 4:23: "And be renewed in the spirit of your minds."

Isaiah 43:18-19: "Do not remember the former things, or consider the things of old. I am about to do a new thing; now it springs forth, do you not perceive it? I will make a way in the wilderness and rivers in the desert."

Matthew 7:7-8: "Ask, and it will be given you; search, and you will find; knock, and the door will be opened for you. For everyone who asks receives, and everyone who searches finds, and for everyone who knocks, the door will be opened."

Matthew 6:33: "But strive first for the kingdom of God and his righteousness, and all these things will be given to you as well."

Romans 8:11: "If the Spirit of him who raised Jesus from the dead dwells in you, he who raised Christ from the dead will give life to your mortal bodies also through his Spirit that dwells in you."

Romans 8:38-39: "For I am convinced that neither death, nor life, nor angels, nor rulers, nor things present, nor things to come, nor powers, nor height, nor depth, nor anything else in all creation, will be able to separate us from the love of God in Christ Jesus our Lord."

1 Corinthians 2:9: "But, as it is written, 'What no eye has seen, nor ear heard, nor the human heart conceived, what God has prepared for those who love him.'"

Luke 5:36-39: "And no one puts new wine into old wineskins; otherwise, the new wine will burst the skins and will be spilled, and the skins will be destroyed. But new wine must be put into fresh wineskins. And no one after drinking old wine desires new wine, but says, 'The old is good.'"

Isaiah 40:31: "But those who wait for the Lord shall renew their strength, they shall mount up with wings like eagles, they shall run and not be weary, they shall walk and not faint."

Jeremiah 29:11: "For surely I know the plans I have for you, says the Lord, plans for your welfare and not for harm, to give you a future with hope."

Matthew 5:14-16: "You are the light of the world. A city built on a hill cannot be hid. No one after lighting a lamp puts it under the bushel basket, but on the lampstand, and it gives light to all in the house. In the same way, let your light shine before others, so that they may see your good works and give glory to your Father in heaven."

Galatians 2:20: "and it is no longer I who live, but it is Christ who lives in me. And the life I now live in the flesh I live by faith in the Son of God, who loved me and gave himself for me."

James 4:8: "Draw near to God, and he will draw near to you. Cleanse your hands, you sinners, and purify your hearts, you double-minded."

1 Peter 2:9: "But you are a chosen race, a royal priesthood, a holy nation, God's own people, in order that you may proclaim the mighty acts of him who called you out of darkness into his marvelous light."

Ephesians 1:4-5: "Just as he chose us in Christ before the foundation of the world to be holy and blameless before him in love. He destined us for adoption as his children through Jesus Christ, according to the good pleasure of his will."

Acts 17:28: "For 'In him we live and move and have our being'; as even some of your own poets have said, 'For we too are his offspring.'"

Matthew 9:17: "Neither is new wine put into old wineskins; otherwise, the skins burst, and the wine is spilled, and the skins are destroyed; but new wine is put into fresh wineskins, and so both are preserved."

2 Corinthians 5:17: "So if anyone is in Christ, there is a new creation: everything old has passed away; see, everything has become new!"

Psalm 85:6: "Will you not revive us again, so that your people may rejoice in you?"

Psalm 119:25: "My soul clings to the dust; revive me according to your word."

Hosea 6:1-2: "Come, let us return to the Lord; for it is he who has torn, and he will heal us; he has struck down, and he will bind us up. After two days he will revive us; on the third day he will raise us up, that we may live before him."

Psalm 119:37: "Turn my eyes from looking at vanities; give me life in your ways."

Psalm 23:3: "He restores my soul. He leads me in right paths for his name's sake."

Ephesians 2:10: "For we are what he has made us, created in Christ Jesus for good works, which God prepared beforehand to be our way of life."

Philippians 3:8-9: "I regard everything as loss because of the surpassing value of knowing Christ Jesus my Lord. For his sake I have suffered the loss of all things, and I regard them as rubbish, in order that I may gain Christ and be found in him, not having a righteousness of my own that comes from the law, but one that comes through faith in Christ, the righteousness from God based on faith."

2 Timothy 1:7: "for God did not give us a spirit of cowardice, but rather a spirit of power and of love and of self-discipline."

Romans 12:1: "I appeal to you therefore, brothers and sisters, by the mercies of God, to present your bodies as a living sacrifice, holy and acceptable to God, which is your spiritual worship."

Notes

Initial

_____

_____

_____

_____

_____

_____

_____

_____

_____

_____

_____

_____

Later

_____

_____

_____

_____

_____

THIS IS NOT A CONCLUSION

BEYOND THE VEIL: THE INTIMATE REVOLUTION OF DIVINE LOVE

You have come so far. And if you have truly begun to walk out this journey, you already know your life will never be the same. In fact, your life is beginning to bloom into its original design. You've only just begun.

And now you are ready to hear the truth.

I hope it is not too much for you to take. But here we go...

Growth does not come easy.

And radical metamorphosis doesn't come without a price.

Imagine being a simple caterpillar, leading a simple life, when a deep and mysterious urge starts to stir within you. This isn't the predictable rhythm of hunger compelling you to munch on simple leaves. It's a call to something greater, a gentle whisper beckoning you toward a destiny you can hardly fathom. You heed this irresistible call, surrendering to the unknown, encasing yourself in a self-made cocoon, a chrysalis. Your world shrinks to this tiny space, a womb of sorts, fostering the birth of something extraordinary.

What follows is a period of profound stillness, a pause in the rush of your life, but beneath this tranquil façade, a radical and pulsing transformation is underway. Your caterpillar form dissolves into goo. What you thought you were breaks down into a cellular soup. You have let go of all that you were so that you can become all that you can be. This is the stage of dissolution where the old is dismantled to make way for the new.

For you aren't adding on to what you were. You are becoming what you were always intended to be. And from this seeming chaos ... a new order, a new life form begins to emerge.

Slowly, from this gooey mass, the beginnings of your new form take shape. Limbs are generated, wings develop, and intricate patterns etch themselves onto your body. The transformation is breathtaking, nothing short of a miracle. Soon, the lowly caterpillar is no more. In its place, an exquisite butterfly waits to make its debut.

But this journey isn't complete yet. One last hurdle stands in your way - the chrysalis that has been your sanctuary is now a barrier to your freedom. You must break free. This struggle tests your strength and perseverance. Each push against the hardened shell, each strain of your new muscles, is arduous but necessary. This struggle doesn't weaken you. It fortifies you, and strengthens you, preparing you for the vast world that awaits.

And then, finally, you break through! The cocoon splits open, a triumphant testament to your perseverance. You emerge, a creature of profound beauty, ready to embrace the skies. Your wings, a dazzling spectacle of colors and patterns, flutter tentatively. You have evolved, transformed, and are now ready to take flight.

And on the air, the very breath of God that has existed since physical time began, the same air that God breathed into Adam's lungs, your wings flutter and are stirred to flight.

Like the butterfly, you are a testament to the power of transformation, the intent of God's design of unending potential for growth and change. Your journey echoes a timeless lesson - that through intimacy and perseverance, we break free from our old design, rise from our challenges, and soar toward our true potential in Christ.

As you take your first flight, you are not just a beautiful new creation. You are a symbol of hope and renewal. And you can never go back to crawling on the ground again. You have not been revived. You have not been repurposed. And this process is not an add-on to the old you. You have been revolutionized through a new understanding of yourself, of your Father, and of your Husband.

You are a Bride in gleaming white, staring the Bridegroom in the eyes, face to face.

And there is no veil between you.

The Spotless Bride

We are told in 2 Corinthians 10:5 that we must take every thought captive.

This is not an option. It is a requirement.

Even though you are beginning this journey of intimacy, and there is no going back, you will have a world that tries to tell you that you are still what you were. Every day you must renew your mind, cast your sights upon heavenly things, and walk in the true reality of your identity. And when hardship strikes, when the world feels unforgiving, you must gaze into the depths of your Beloved's eyes. In His gaze, you will see a reflection of your true essence, a portrait of who you are. His eyes, always radiant with His love for you, will remind you of your intrinsic worth. It is there, in the gaze of your Divine Bridegroom, that you will always discover your true identity, unmasked and beautiful.

For every day, to your Bridegroom, is your wedding day. And you are always spotless on that day, no matter how far you think you have fallen.

And to illustrate this, I want to tell you one last personal story.

Back in 2009, my fiancée and I lived in New Orleans. But as our wedding date was fast approaching and our families lived in North Carolina, we decided to marry closer to home.

The week before our wedding, we made the drive from New Orleans to North Carolina, traveling through Louisiana, Mississippi, Alabama, Georgia, and South Carolina to get to Raleigh, NC. If you have never done this drive before, it's extraordinarily boring, a mindless 13-hour drive of the wide-open interstate with little to stare at other than trees and drivers in other vehicles with equally glazed expressions.

And for the initial portion of the drive, my wife took the lead.

Now the rental car we were using had no cruise control. And my wife, God bless her, has a lead foot.

And we were in a hurry.

And right off the bat of this 13-hour drive, my wife proceeded to get two speeding tickets in two different states - Mississippi and Alabama. Needless to say, we had a little argument, and I took over the driving.

But after ten hours of driving, I became a bit tired, so she takes back over.

And she proceeds to race right into a speed trap, picking up her third ticket in three different states on the same day.

You can imagine, it was a little bit ... tense. We had already blown our budget with the wedding, and my soon-to-be-wife has picked up three speeding tickets in states we didn't live! I'm mad, she's mad, and we're both freaking out. I'm calculating the thousands of dollars in lawyers' fees we will have to pay to be represented in multiple states around the same time period. And I'm also wondering how much our combined insurance rate will exponentially increase over the next five years. It wasn't looking good. And, oh yeah, there's still a wedding to pay for!

After arriving in North Carolina, we had a week with family and friends we hadn't seen in years. But the whole time, I'm trying to figure out how we're going to pay this debt we're racking up.

And then comes the wedding day.

And as I'm standing there in front of the audience, on a beautiful lake on a perfect weather day, with my best men next to me, and next to my dad who is presiding over the wedding, I take a deep breath when the music changes.

And there she is, at the end of the aisle.

I can't begin to describe how beautiful she was. How beautiful she is. I was completely undone with her presence, as she stood at the end of the aisle next to her father, who was giving his oldest daughter, his most precious gift, to me.

It is an incredible, surreal, feeling; to see someone who is promising their heart to you, and holding your heart in their hands, giving themself completely to you, and you to them, as they walk towards you.

There is no feeling like it. And I had tears for sure. Even now, writing this, envisioning her walking towards me, the tears come right back!

Blameless. Spotless. Perfect.

So let me ask you. At that moment, standing there, do you think there was a single thought of those three speeding tickets, or any other argument we'd ever had? Those tickets were the farthest thing from my mind, completely removed from that place and the holiness of that moment when my wife and I became one before the eyes of the world and God.

But it would still be years before I understood what it meant to see myself through Heavenly eyes.

Almost three years after our wedding, I had an up close and personal encounter with a man/God named Jesus. And I began a journey with Him.

It was quite bumpy at first.

And much like you, part of my struggle in my growing relationship with Christ was coming out of the guilt, shame, and condemnation of my past – drug addiction, witchcraft, sorcery, hedonism, and even death. My life before Christ was painted with the most terrible of brushes. And my self-worth dragged its bloody knuckles on the rockiest of sharp terrain.

No matter how much of the goodness of the Lord I heard about, no matter what I read about, I could not shake my past. And I couldn't quite get over the hump. This guilt of my old life and who I used to be was this terrible weight around my neck, tighter than a millstone dragging me into the depths. It manifested in anxiety, hyper-critical thinking, and anger that would erupt at the worst of times.

In 2014, my wife and I welcomed our precious daughter into the world. And like many married couples with their first child, our priorities shifted in ways you don't think about sans kids. We needed real and substantial income, so I took a job in high-risk commission-only corporate sales. And while I was making more money than my wife and I had seen in a long time, I was struggling. The stress of the job was incredible. The difference in ramen noodles or filet mignon for the month was literally single-digit sales, and there was no safety net if I didn't close my clients.

But the Lord remained faithful. Immediately I rocketed to the top of the company, finding favor left and right, earning salesman of the month awards multiple times.

Yet, I was still filled with nerve-wracking fear, leading to debilitating panic attacks. I felt that at any moment, everything would fall apart like a house of cards. That I would fail my growing family. That I wasn't good enough. No matter how many honors I gained, no matter how many sales I closed, and no matter how many new client accounts were created, I would sometimes sit under my office desk, gripped with overwhelming fear. I had constant nightmares of not earning enough and losing my job, that my wife would leave me, and that my child would grow up with some other father that could provide more financial security. And these were silly dreams that I knew had no basis in reality. I knew my wife would never leave me. I knew that I would always do whatever was necessary for my children. But the anxiety was unrelenting. And no matter how many books I read, or prayed, or sought counseling, nothing helped.

And it went without saying that I never thought I would measure up to what Jesus had called me to. I knew that I heard the voice of God. I had seen Him with my physical eyes. I had traveled around the world on missions. I had prayed for and had seen major miracles in Jesus' name. I had spoken in front of churches, led worship, gave sacrificially of my money and time, and served faithfully. I knew there was a call on my life.

And still, I was filled with crippling fear.

No matter what I did to prove myself in my own eyes, I felt that at any moment, my entire life would be yanked from me, leaving me with nothing except my failure and shame.

Until one night, when I was praying and asking for forgiveness and mercy for the millionth time, I heard a still small voice speak over the cacophony of other voices in my head. It was a voice that came from my heart that said *"Ken, do you remember your wedding when you saw your wife coming down the aisle? Do you remember the lump in your throat, the tears in your eyes? Do you remember how when you saw her all you could think of was your love for her? You didn't think about speeding tickets or arguments or your finances. All you could think about was how amazing she was, how beautiful, how precious, how vulnerable, how loved. And how much she loved you. And that she would never leave, and always stand by you. Do you remember?"*

I remember nodding, and immediately I was taken back to my wedding day, standing across from my wife in her radiant glory before me, a soft smile on her face, and gazing into my eyes.

And then I heard His voice again, nudging me from my memories. *"Ken, how you looked at your wife coming down the aisle and standing before you is how I've looked at you since you were conceived in the Father's mind."*

And just like that, the voice of many waters became a roar that washed over my mind, body, and spirit, forcing the other intrusive voices into silence, and hardly ever to return again.

We are the bride.

And He is the bridegroom, waiting for you to take the walk towards Him.

Our world suffers because we do not see ourselves or Him through His eyes. The love of a Husband for His bride.

We are in union. And we are born again anew every day.

For eternity.

The Call to Intimacy

My prayer is that you hear these words of your new beginning, a call to a deeper relationship with God, an invitation to voyage into the vast sea of His love and faith. This call is beckoning you across the illusory boundary separating the physical from the spiritual, inviting you into a journey to uncover His mysteries that have lain just beyond our understanding.

You are a treasured jewel in the grand scheme of creation. The Father's love for you is unyielding, and His watchful care ever present, your life serving as a testimony to His endless benevolence. Like the stars and planets that illuminate the night sky, you have the unlimited potential to shine with God's love and bring heaven to earth through your connection with Him.

Your relationship with God is not a solitary endeavor, but a sacred partnership flourishing with mutual adoration. And you will find that as you plunge deeper into this relationship, your heart syncs with Jesus' symphony of love echoing throughout the universe, every note resonating with God's love encompassing you.

Your heart becomes a sacred cup, filled to the brim with Jesus' love that naturally spills over to those around you. And in this pouring out of this new wine, you manifest a sliver of heaven on earth, even in the darkest prisons, just as Paul and Silas. Your actions, words, and thoughts bear witness to this divine love and your intimate bond with God.

Like a tree planted by streams of water, your spiritual roots delve into the depths, drawing nourishment from Wisdom. And your branches stretch towards Heaven, revealing to those who know how to see, your spiritual growth. As you thrive in God's light, you bear fruits of love, joy, peace, patience, kindness, goodness, faithfulness, gentleness, and self-control, which you will generously share with the world.

You're no longer an observer in the tapestry of life. You're the needle wielded in the hands of the most Perfect Artist, guided by the Perfect Model, threading love and light into the cosmic weave. Through your communion with God, you are a vessel of His peace, a beacon of His love, and a mirror of His grace.

Heed the call.

Fall into deeper oceans of intimacy.

Embrace the journey, the revelations, and the transformation.

Unravel the revealed mystery *behind* the veil. Immerse yourself in God's infinite love. And witness the slice of heaven you bring to earth with every heartbeat pulsing with love.

The Revolution of Heart and Mind

As these words drenched in Scripture echo into the deepest places of your heart, they beckon you towards revolution. Not a revolution of conflict and upheaval, but a revolution of heart and mind - *spiritual metamorphosis*.

This is not the time to let the comfort of the familiar limit your exploration of the Presence you feel all around you. Let Him overwhelm and inspire you to seek a greater measure of God. Feel the expansion of the horizon, venture beyond the safety of what you know, and embrace the dynamic dance with God. Seek not only to listen to His word but to understand and embody it, allowing it to shape your interactions with the world, mold your perceptions, and guide your actions.

Take on the mantle of His love, for the yoke is easy and the burden is light, and let it redefine your understanding of others. Begin to see them not as the world sees them but as Christ sees them - as beloved treasures, precious in His sight, worth the ultimate sacrifice. Each individual is an embodiment of God's creative power, a unique tapestry of experiences, emotions, and thoughts, woven together into a singular narrative that adds to the grand story of existence.

I urge you to not hold back on this journey of transformation. Allow His mind, thoughts, and ways to permeate every facet of your life, altering your perspective, deepening your relationships, and transforming your understanding of Him. Explore the depths of God's love, mercy, and grace. And in the process, you'll find that your capacity for empathy, kindness, and compassion grows exponentially.

And you will find that as this transformation takes place, you'll begin to reflect and shine with Christ's love more clearly, becoming a beacon of His light in a world that often dwells in shadows. You'll start to see Christ in others, and they'll see Christ in you. And in this process, you will find that you are not just a Christian going through the motions. You won't just be a simple follower. You are becoming a tangible manifestation of His love and grace.

Embrace this revolution, this journey of spiritual metamorphosis. Venture beyond the comfortable, explore your dynamic and ever-moving relationship with God, and start to see others as Christ sees them. Moving beyond the veil isn't just about transforming your faith. It is about transforming your life, and through your actions, transforming the world around you.

For it's in your transformation that you truly begin to live as Christ intended - filled with love, infused with grace, and reflecting His divine image to the world.

A Final Invitation

You have not reached the end.

This simple guide is just a glimmer of an eternity of beginnings, of moving deeper into realms of intimacy with the Creator of the universe every day. And it is a new beginning every day, where you will spend eternities gazing at the wonder of the One who not only put the stars into motion but created you to share them with.

Chapter 4 of The Book of Revelation offers a breathtaking glimpse of God's throne room, where mysterious creatures with six wings hold court before Him exclaiming *Holy, holy, holy, the Lord God the Almighty, who was and is and is to come.*

And like the author of Revelation, you are invited to *Come up here* into this moment. After all, we are seated in Christ in Heavenly places.

Like John of Patmos, who entered into the spirit and into the throne room of His Grace, you too are allowed to step into the profound intimacy of this eternal moment the same way.

This is a space you enter into with your heart and not your head. It is through the Secret Place and your intimate love with Jesus that you can stand boldly before this throne. Not by your work or efforts, but by Christ alone who offered Himself fully for you, his Bride.

All you had to do was say YES.

And being before this throne, in the spirit, you realize this isn't a distant, impersonal seat of power; it is the epicenter of infinite love, the heart of the cosmos, and the locus of the profound relationship you share with the Divine.

Surrounding God's throne are the twenty-four elders, dressed in gleaming white, and wearing gold crowns. And every time the mysterious creatures sing out their praises to God, the elders cast their crowns at God's feet and sing *out You are worthy, our Lord and God, to receive glory and honor and power, for you created all things, and by your will they existed and were created!*

And the stunning realization flows over you as you realize who Jesus learned His servant's heart from. For Jesus is His Father's child, the firstborn of God, and Jesus did the work of a Father who loves, who doesn't exist to be worshiped *but is worshiped because He exists and is worthy.*

Haven't you ever wondered how the crowns get back onto the heads of the elders after they toss them at God's beautiful feet?

Our God restores all things. And He passionately loves his creation, continually restoring His creations to the Glory He calls them to.

So, my friend, heed the call of intimacy and of Revelation 4 - *Come up here.* Let your heart resonate with this divine frequency and ascend to greater intimacy with God.

The celestial door stands open for you, free of separation and its torn veil.

All you must do is step through.

And I will see you on the other side.

Notes

Initial

_____

_____

_____

_____

_____

_____

_____

_____

_____

_____

_____

_____

Later

_____

_____

_____

_____

_____

About the Author

Ken Arrington's passion is to see people re-awaken to their rightful birthright, authority, and inheritance as children of God through the love of Jesus. A husband, father, and licensed pastor in multiple countries, Ken currently serves full-time overseas and directs a UK-registered charity that provides hope and support for the neglected, in-need, trafficked, and addicted, while also planting regional houses of prayer and worship.

Ken also works as a content creator who desires to reveal the beauty of Jesus and a deeper understanding of the Bible, offering over 18 hours of online courses. Ken has ghost-written numerous historical reviews, books, and articles for publishers worldwide. And when he isn't teaching or with his family on wild God adventures, you can often find him on social media designing videos that offer a little history, a little mystery, and a lot of Jesus.

Made in the USA
Middletown, DE
05 November 2023

42003616R00096